GIVE US THIS DAY

GIVE US THIS DAY

by

Ken Stallard

Author of
Road to Nowhere

Published by
ARTHUR JAMES LIMITED

THE DRIFT EVESHAM WORCS.
WR11 4NW

First Edition 1979

British Library Cataloguing in Publication Data
Stallard, Ken
Give us this day.
1. Christian life
I. Title
248 BV4501.2

ISBN 0-85305-206-9

Text set in 11/12 pt Photon Baskerville, printed by photolithography, and bound in Great Britain at The Pitman Press, Bath

DEDICATION

Dedicated to the Glory of God in thankfulness for the great things He is doing, and in loving memory of Dad and Shane who contributed so much and were called so suddenly.

CONTENTS

1

STRENGTH MADE PERFECT IN WEAKNESS

I DIDN'T WANT Roy Wilson to die. I stood beside the hospital bed and looked through the transparent oxygen tent which covered the very still body. His face was very pale, the eyes were closed and there was little evidence of the fact that he was still breathing.

Tubes appeared to be everywhere, up the nose, at the side of the mouth and at the wrist. A bottle containing a colourless liquid was suspended at the head of the bed and I felt Roy's life was ebbing away, drip by drip, similar to the liquid which was slowly dribbling into the motionless form lying on the bed.

As I stood there I silently prayed for Roy. I couldn't understand why this lad, only twenty years of age, should want to choose suicide.

Who can fathom what goes on in a mind tortured by the loss of a loved one, or feel the pangs of a broken heart overwhelmed with shock and unspeakable grief?

In Roy's case it was a double tragedy. Fay, his girl friend of two years standing, had suddenly and quite unexpectedly called off their engagement in favour of one of Roy's best friends. Then, during a short period in which Roy tried by all means to win back her love, his father had a severe heart attack and died.

Roy had been a pillar of strength to his widowed mother from the minute his father died until a couple of weeks after the funeral. He was an only child and he knew his mother, a sickly woman at the best of times, was completely bowled over by this sudden bereavement in the family. He too, felt keenly the loss of his father, whom he loved dearly, and tried hard to support his mother in this time of crisis.

Then just two weeks after the funeral something snapped inside the lad. Bouts of depression and a feeling of loneliness was often followed by floods of tears. As the days went by the tears and depressions increased until quite early one morning his mother found him collapsed in a heap at the bottom of the stairs.

The family doctor diagnosed a deep sense of shock to the nervous system and prescribed two kinds of tablets. A further two weeks elapsed and the boy's mother found him unconscious in bed. He had taken all the tablets which remained, plus some aspirins he had found in the house. An ambulance was called and Roy was whisked off to the local hospital where he received emergency treatment and a stomach pump.

Mother and son were personal friends of mine, apart from the fact that Roy was a member of one of my Mission Youth Clubs. I had spent a lot of hours in the company of this family in an attempt to bring as much cheer and practical help as possible.

In the short time following the death of Mr. Wilson, both Mrs. Wilson and Roy had unburdened their griefs to me and began to look upon me as one of the family, especially as their nearest relatives lived a long way off.

It was not unusual, therefore, for Mrs. Wilson, who was almost at her wits end, to 'phone me in these present circumstances and I left immediately to join her at the hospital.

I continued to watch Roy, looking for the slightest sign of movement. Oh why didn't he yawn or move or even twitch?

I stood, feeling quite helpless, until I remembered to pray. I have seen dozens of miracles and not the least of these have been miracles of healing. Each miracle had followed a period of prayer and now I could only pray.

My prayer was silent as Mrs. Wilson tip-toed to my side. Neither of us spoke since I felt she understood what I was doing.

Suddenly she clutched my arm. "Look," she whispered, "he has moved."

The right hand had been clenched almost tightly, now the fingers were extended as they lay on the counterpane. I willed the hand to move again but it did not, but I was quick to notice a definite pulsating of a vein on the back of it, and inwardly I told myself that where there was life there was hope.

Mrs. Wilson and I were allowed to stay another twenty minutes and then it was necessary for me to leave for another pressing appointment.

I couldn't get the lad off my mind as I left the hospital. The mother, so small and frail, was a pathetic figure of loneliness and grief; and as I drove away her words kept ringing in my ears, "If I lose my son I shall have nothing left at all."

Somehow I was very early for my next appointment and this gave me the opportunity of lifting up Mrs. Wilson and Roy in Prayer. I asked for some measure of comfort from God's Word and with anticipation reached for my Bible.

Minutes later, I knew it was not by accident that I alighted on the seventh chapter of St. Luke where I read that Jesus and many of his disciples went into a city called Nain. When they arrived at the gate of the city they came across a funeral procession. A widow was taking her only son to be buried.

When Jesus saw the grief of the mother, He had compassion on her and spoke two words of comfort, "Weep not."

"Weep not," the very meaning of these words were the last I had uttered only minutes before at the hospital! I had tried to get Mrs. Wilson to dry her eyes and left her with some words of comfort, now here in the Bible was almost an identical situation. The widow, the grief and the only son all followed the same pattern.

I eagerly read on. Jesus said, "Young man, I say unto thee, Arise. And he that was dead sat up, and began to speak. And Jesus delivered him to his mother."

When I read those words a kind of peace fell upon my soul. There clearly written was the fact that Jesus had restored a dead man to his widowed mother. I knew that the power of Jesus Christ is the same today as it was then and what He did in this instance He could certainly do for Mrs. Wilson and Roy.

It was almost time for that appointment of mine now, so I offered a prayer of thanks to the Lord for leading me to this passage of Scripture. And as I thanked Him I asked that He might be pleased to perform the same miracle at the hospital. I left it at that.

That very night Mrs. Wilson telephoned from home. How different she sounded from the last time I had spoken to her only hours previously.

"Ken, our prayers have been answered," she began, "Roy has regained consciousness and knew I was there! The doctor seems very hopeful now that he is going to be all right but never left me in any doubt that he has had a very near escape from death. Will you come to the hospital again tomorrow?"

I did visit Roy the next day and at intervals during the next couple of weeks. He quickly recovered and was allowed to go home where he found help and loving care.

By and by he met up with a very nice girl and eventually got married. I lost a good Mission Youth Club member but he found a new type of happiness, and for the mother's part, I knew she had found a new type of faith.

I often shared with them the Scripture the Lord had shared with me that crisis day. They came to realise that He is the Christ of every crisis and the One who meets the deepest need.

I was sure that the One who had met their need that day would continue to meet their needs every day of their lives. I know that thus far they have proved it to be so.

2

CASTING THE NET

TIM HAD a real drink problem. Although only just sixteen he had all the appearances of someone two or three years older and so easily passed as being of age for frequenting public houses.

There were few nights that he missed going out for alcohol and on each occasion he got himself drunk.

The manual job he was employed on paid well so that he could afford the drink, and this coupled with the fact that his older friends encouraged the habit, did little to alleviate his problem.

On the one hand Tim craved for drink, but on the other he was regularly filled with remorse and continually promised himself that he would moderate the habit.

Although he tried hard in his endeavours to stop drinking, he always lost. He came occasionally to the Mission Youth Club, usually the worse for drink when he arrived, or he left early to become so.

Then one evening Tim arrived at the Club with his right hand heavily bandaged.

During a very drunken spell he had seen his own reflection in a plate glass window, and feeling sickened at what he saw, he lashed at the glass with a clenched fist. Consequently he cut a main tendon in the hand which caused his little finger to droop and to become helpless. Furthermore, he had lost all grip in the hand.

Although I could tell this lad was extremely worried about the hand he tried to make light of it, and, went around the Club showing other members the scar and stitches beneath the bandaged splint.

Within minutes of Tim showing me the hand and telling me

his story, the electric ring on which I was making toast suddenly went out.

"It looks as though your cooker has burnt out, Ken." This from Ern, another youth member who sat on the steps which led down to the kitchen. "If you have got a screwdriver I will fix the plug for you."

I fished out a small pair of scissors in lieu of a screwdriver and handed these to Ern to tackle the job.

He quickly unscrewed the plug and found the wires inside had completely burnt out.

"Look, here's your trouble" he explained and showed me that the plug only contained a lot of black dust where wires had once been.

Just then I was kneeling before the cupboard to fetch out some cups from the back of it when I heard an inner voice say to me quite clearly, "Put the plug together," and, before I realised it I had repeated those words.

"It's no good putting it back together like that," snorted Ern in disgust, "I shall have to cut off some more wires." "Put the plug together," I said it again quite authoritatively this time, and Ern did as he was told and with a withering look threw the lead on the table.

Again I heard the voice speak within me, "Put the plug in the socket on the other side," and, as before, I repeated the words indicating that the plug should be put in a socket on the other side of the kitchen wall.

At this Ern was quite indignant and looked at me as though I was out of my mind.

"It's no good putting it in another socket," he said, "the trouble is in the plug."

"Go on, put it in the other socket," I urged and the lad did so with an exaggerated sigh.

Instantly the ring began to glow again!

Ern's face was a study. "I don't know!" he exclaimed shaking his head, "how did that happen?"

I smiled and said, "I'm plugged into the Chief Electrician,

Ern, and He performs miracles!" Ern laughed but he instantly knew I was talking about God.

I've seen several miracles happen like this in the Club, and I believe the Lord uses them to open up a way to speak for Him and to show He is still a miracle working God.

In this instance I was able to speak from St. John, Chapter 21.

The disciples had gone out fishing all night but had caught nothing. In the morning Jesus stood on the shore and enquired about their catch. When they had told Him they had caught nothing, Jesus said, "Cast the net on the right side of the ship, and ye shall find."

The disciples did as they were instructed and found they could not draw the net in now because of the multitude of fish.

What was different? The sea was the same, the fishermen and the fishing technique was the same.

It was abundantly clear to me that the presence of God's power went to work the minute the net was put on the right side of the ship, and likewise at our Mission Youth Club, the same power went into the electric ring when the plug was put on the other side of the wall. Electric power through black dust just had to be a miracle!

When I got home to bed I prayed and thanked the Lord for the miracle. As I prayed I received a further two words which were simply "Tim's hand!" As I found myself praying for the lad's injured hand, light promptly dawned upon my soul. I knew that God had shown me something even more wonderful!

If He could bring power through a dead plug to cause an electric ring to glow, by the same power He could work through Tim's dead tendon to give life in that helpless hand.

I was so excited with this revelation that I could hardly wait for the next Club session to arrive.

As soon as I saw Tim I told him about my experience with the Lord but his reaction was not very favourable and he openly scoffed at the idea.

I asked him if I could pray there and then over the hand and he reluctantly agreed. When I finished praying I asked him to put his fingers around my wrist and to squeeze it as hard as he could.

"You know I can't," he complained, "I've got no grip in that hand at all."

"Go on, just try," I urged, and he put a very limp hand on my wrist.

"Now squeeze it."

"I can't."

"Go on, squeeze it as hard as you can."

Tim's fingers curled around my wrist and they trembled slightly as he tried to put pressure on them. The hold was very weak and then I felt it getting firmer and firmer still. Within seconds his grip was beginning to hurt my wrist and I watched a wide grin spread over his face.

He relaxed his fingers and started to stretch and clench them again looking at them very intently all the time.

"It's a lot better," he pronounced and went off to demonstrate what his hand could do to his mates.

It was plain to see that Tim could grip now but I couldn't understand why the finger still appeared to be dead.

I promised Tim I would pray on but several weeks passed before he came to the Club again. When he returned he had not been in the village hall five minutes before the electric ring failed again. The only time it had done so since that first experience. And, by a further miracle, it suddenly began to glow again too.

I drew Tim's attention to the electric ring again but this time he was too keen to collect friends for drinking than to be prayed for. He left the hall with a drooping finger still.

As in the case of the electric fire, God has often spoken to me through material things.

I was sad that Tim had gone off with that drooping finger when I believed God was going to do something for it. After all He had given strength to the hand. But I wasn't left to be sad for long because as I sat by the fire after all the members had left the hall, I had my usual time of private prayer and reading. I felt the Presence of The Lord very near as I was drawn to the 58th Chapter of Isaiah and read:

"Then shall thy light break forth as the morning, and thine health shall spring forth speedily: and thy righteousness shall go before thee; the glory of the Lord shall be thy reward.

"Then shalt thou call, and the Lord shall answer; thou shalt cry, and He shall say, Here I am. If thou take away from the midst of thee the yoke, the putting forth of the finger, and speaking vanity;

"And if thou draw out thy soul to the hungry, and satisfy the afflicted soul; then shall thy light rise in obscurity, and thy darkness be as the noonday:

"And the Lord shall guide thee continually, and satisfy thy soul in drought, and make fat thy bones: and thou shalt be like a watered garden, and like a spring of water, whose waters fail not."

Those comforting words were all I needed. Little texts from that brief reading seemed to jump from the page and hit me.

"Thy light break forth as the morning," what a picture this was of the electric ring. "The Lord shall answer," what a positive promise this was, and then "Take away from the midst of thee the yoke." Tim's yoke was the drink problem but I knew the Power of God could dispense with that. And then the actual mention of the finger, for it was clearly written in verse 9 of the Chapter "the putting forth of the finger."

I was now fully convinced that God was able to give Tim the power to lift that lifeless finger so that his experience would be like the "satisfying of the soul in drought, and be like a watered garden, whose waters fail not."

The last time I saw Tim was about a month ago when I picked him up as he was hitch-hiking home from work. I asked how the finger was and he said, "not much better" but I couldn't help noticing how he lifted it up as he replied. He was on his way home from heavy manual work on a building site so

I knew the hand was no longer a handicap to him.

I dropped Tim near his home and as I drove away I thought of a verse from Mat. 21, "This is the Lord's doing, and it is marvellous in our eyes."

3

BROUGHT FROM THE BRINK OF DEATH

THE LITTLE LADY wept bitterly all through the service I was taking at a small village Baptist Church. I was concerned and at the close of the meeting asked her if there was anything I could do to help relieve her stress.

"It's my little grandson," she began, "he is dying and is probably already dead."

It didn't take long for her to pour out her story. The grandson was two years old and had contracted a rare virus. He had been admitted to an isolation ward in a nearby hospital and his condition had worsened by the hour.

"My son and his wife were told that the virus could be fatal," she added, "and early this morning they were summoned to the hospital and I have not seen them since."

It was a gloomy tale she had to tell and when she had presented the facts of the case, it certainly sounded as though a miracle would be needed to save the little lad.

"There is nothing we can do, " she said a couple of times between sobs before I was moved to say, "We can pray."

I asked if we might pray together and she nodded. She was unable to pray audibly now because of the extent of her weeping so I gently began to pray aloud for the lad and for her.

As I prayed, the earnestness and the gravity of the situation tugged at my soul so that my prayer became fervent. I pleaded with the Lord for the boy's life and then quite clearly I heard a voice speaking to my heart. "This sickness is not unto death." It was as clear as a bell.

My joy was uncontrollable and yet unexplainable. I felt as though I wanted to laugh and cry at the same time. I was flooded with relief and all tension had left my body. My previous feeling of concern had simply passed away.

"The little chap is going to be all right, I just know it," I said, but the little lady was still sniffing a lot and dabbing at her eyes with her handkerchief. She was not convinced.

As I drove home, I sang to myself with sheer delight. I had heard God's voice and there was no shadow of doubt in my mind that the child was to be healed, and the lady's grief turned into joy.

My prayers that night and the next morning were expressions of praise and thanksgiving to God. I didn't have to pray for the little boy's health because the Lord had already dealt with it.

I went to my secular job with floods of joy which soon became obvious to my colleagues at the office. One of them ventured to ask why I was so radiantly happy and I explained about the incident of the previous evening and my conviction of the healing of the child.

But many friends are not content with faith only, but continually look for confirming facts. My colleague was one of these.

"Why don't you ring the hospital and see how he is," she suggested, "you will know then if he is any better or worse."

I remembered how the Lord had said to me "This sickness is not unto death," and He never makes mistakes. I also recalled these were the very words Jesus said when Mary and Martha had sent to Him the message that their brother Lazarus was sick.

In that instance Jesus recalled Lazarus from the grave and by a similar miracle He could heal our little boy. After all He is the same Lord!

My colleague lingered by my side as I telephoned the hospital and was put in touch with the ward sister.

"All I can say it's a miracle," the sister began, "last night he was extremely ill but he suddenly took a turn for the better. Would you believe it if I told you he is now as bright as a button and playing with a ball with one of the nurses?"

Yes I did believe it, of course! The sister said it was a miracle and often quotations about miracles are expressed without the quoter realising the truth of the quote.

I have no other explanation for it but the miracle working of God.

This story with a happy ending occurred just before Easter and within a few days the grandmother sent me an Easter card. In it she said she really belonged to another denomination but she had felt drawn to the Baptist Church where I was preaching that night when she was so distressed. "Our prayers were answered," she wrote, "and Billy came home on Thursday. I must say I've not seen anything like that before."

The people in St. Mark, Chapter 2 were similarly amazed when one sick of the palsy was healed before them. Their words were similar too for they said, "We never saw it on this fashion."

The answer lies in the Epistle of James, Chapter 5, "The effectual fervent prayer of a righteous man availeth much."

4

LEARNING TO TRUST

THIRTY-TWO OF us young airmen sat in the classroom of R.A.F. Credenhill, Hereford, and heard our clerk provisioning instructor say, "This is the last course I shall be teaching before I leave the Service. I have never had a hundred per cent pass and I want you to work hard so that I can fulfil that ambition before I leave."

I intended to work hard and practice my new found Christian faith at the same time. I had been converted just five days before I joined up for National Service and had just completed eight weeks square-bashing. Now, at Hereford, we were in for trade training and subsequent posting to a permanent Station.

The course lasted ten weeks and I soon came to realise that every one of my prayers was being answered. My new faith in God was strengthened as I felt He was helping me in all the new and strange things I had to learn.

Mock tests were held at regular intervals and I passed each one of these with flying colours. I studied hard and was confident that God would bring me successfully through the final exams as I had already committed my three year service engagement to Him. I repeatedly asked for His guidance and blessing on my R.A.F. career.

The final exams came and went and I felt I had done very well indeed. We eagerly awaited the results.

I shall never forget standing in a hangar whilst our Commanding Officer climbed up on to a platform to announce those results.

He cleared his throat and began, "This is the very nearest thing we have ever had to a one hundred per cent pass. You worked very hard indeed and only one of you has let us down!"

A short silence followed and we all fidgeted and then he looked straight at me and pointed and said, "You!"

"Stallard is the only one amongst you to fail the course exams."

I was stunned as a murmur ran around the group. I felt humiliated, baffled and sick.

I could not help thinking that I was the only one out of thirty-two airmen to fail the course. What must they be thinking of me? I had let our instructor down too with his hopes of one hundred per cent pass. What would happen to me now?

I was only vaguely aware of all the congratulations which were being poured forth and my eyes smarted as I listened to the postings.

The entire course was being sent home that day on seven days embarkation leave, prior to posting to 401 Air Stores Park at Eindhoven in Holland.

The group dispersed to hand in their kit whilst I stood alone to face the Officer.

"You did so well during the course," he said, "I can only think exam nerves must have let you down."

I said I didn't suffer from nerves and then the course instructor butted in.

"Sir," he began, "Since Stallard did so well on the course would it be possible for him to sit another exam at a later date? I am leaving the R.A.F. in a couple of weeks time and I would be willing to give him some private tuition in between settling up my affairs."

The Officer was not altogether sure this would be allowed but promised to make enquiries, and I was sent back to an empty billet.

That night I lay in my bed and cried. I was the only occupant in a billet which accommodated sixteen beds. All the other beds were empty, mattresses were rolled back and there was a strange silence which pervaded the place.

Later the silence was broken by a violent thunder storm, the rain ran down the windows as the tears dripped down my cheeks.

Why was God so cruel to me? I had prayed hard and taken every opportunity to witness for Him. He had answered all my prayers but why did He have to let me down now when I needed Him most?

I had asked Him to help my career and it seemed obvious that He had allowed me to fail in it miserably.

My faith ebbed and I decided there was not much in Christianity after all.

During the next two weeks I studied alone in a large stuffy classroom. The instructor looked in a couple of times but spent most of his time clearing away his possessions or going off on farewell parties with his mates. One afternoon he stayed just long enough to tell me I would be put into another trade, possibly labouring, if I failed the exam again!

The second exam was similar to the first and I emerged from it feeling just about as confident as the first time.

Some days later I was called before the Commanding Officer who greeted me with, "Stallard, what is the matter with you?"

"Oh no!" I exclaimed, "please don't say I've failed again!"

"Failed," he echoed, "you've passed with such a high mark you put all on that last course to shame!"

I could not understand it but it was impossible to conceal my joy.

"Will I be going to 401 Air Stores Park at Eindhoven? I eagerly enquired, but the Officer shook his head.

"No," he replied, " the Air Ministry, for reasons best known to themselves, have decided to send you to 402 Air Stores Park at Wildenrath in Germany instead."

Within hours I was home on embarkation leave and looking forward to my first trip outside Britain. My enthusiasm, however, was clouded in disappointment when I realised that I would not be joining my other friends from the course.

I eventually found myself standing in front of the Commanding Officer of 402 Air Stores Park at Wildenrath. He was surprised to receive a lone airman and enquired why I had been singled out for the posting.

I explained all about failing the course and concluded by saying, "I am glad I passed the second exam but I must confess I am a little disappointed to be split up from the rest of the course. All my friends are at 401 Air Stores Park at Eindhoven."

"Well they will not be there for much longer," the Commanding Officer smiled, "You obviously do not know that the Unit at Eindhoven is closing and the stores and staff are to be transferred here. Your friends will be rejoining you in a matter of weeks."

I could hardly believe this piece of good news as I was shown into my new office and introduced to a first-class job. I loved the appointment and was blissfully happy with the job from the minute I got to it.

A few weeks later all my course friends arrived from Eindhoven with the transfer of the Unit. Each one was a trained clerk but on arrival at Wildenrath they discovered there were insufficient clerical vacancies. Consequently, several of them went into store work and ended up in sheds.

One of my friends complained bitterly to me one day. "Ken, you were the lucky one," he began, "you were the only one to fail the course and you got the best job of all because you arrived at this Station before us."

By this time I had to admit it wasn't luck, it was clearly a case of God answering my prayers and being with me all the time.

In Romans Chapter 8 I read, "All things work together for good to them that love God, to them who are the called according to His purpose," and in Hebrews 13, "He hath said, I will never leave thee, nor forsake thee."

My thoughts often go back to that night I felt so isolated and heartbroken in the billet. It seemed that God had forsaken me but all the time He was answering my prayers and working His purposes out. He was there all the time!

After three years with the R.A.F. at Wildenrath I earned a very special commendation for meritorious service from the Air Officer Commanding the Second Tactical Air Force, just prior to demob.

It was my twenty-first birthday and hundreds of us were on parade for the A.O.C's annual visit. It was a very proud moment for me when I had to march off the parade ground to receive the commendation.

Yes, the God of all miracles had certainly performed several for me. Receiving the commendation in front of my friends more than compensated for that humiliating experience I had when I was the only one to fail before them. And that experience has always stood as a lesson for me – to trust God implicitly, even when the way is hard and it appears that no answer to prayer is forthcoming.

Faithful is He who promised, "Whatsoever ye shall ask in my Name (JESUS) that will I do, that the Father (GOD) may be glorified in the Son," and "No good thing will He withhold from them that walk uprightly."

5

TOOLS GIVEN FOR THE JOB

I ENTERED MY teens wishing desperately that I could read and write intelligently. My schooling was often interrupted by the frequent move of home.

My father was a farm labourer and changed his job often; consequently we had to leave tied farm cottages and find another home; and for me it was a case of a new class or school too.

I was very conscious of being laughed at because I couldn't form the figure "3". I held the pen so awkwardly that it always came out as the letter "M" and looked more like a bird in flight.

When I left Secondary Modern School at fifteen, I got a job in a grocer's shop but made up my mind that I would try night school in an attempt to improve my English. But this did not turn out very well, due mainly to the fact that I lived four miles from the nearest classes and there was a serious problem with transport at that time too.

Within a couple of years I was attending an inter-denominational Mission and becoming more and more interested in Christian things. It was not very long before all the teaching became relevant to my own life and I was converted as a result of it.

The thing I then desired most, and frequently prayed for, was to be able to read and understand the Bible. I can only say that God did answer those prayers for in a remarkably short space of time I found I had become an avid reader.

I studied the Bible at great length in preparation for local preaching, and I soon came to realise that it was necessary to make notes too. Again, quite remarkably, I found that writing was becoming just as easy as reading, and a year later I was able to go in for a clerical post in the Royal Air Force.

Three years later I returned to civilian life and resumed my Bible studies and local preaching.

About this time I sat in the office at my place of employment and during the hour break for lunch, I began to copy out some Bible texts as I prepared the next Sunday's sermon.

A colleague watched me for some time, and then with a smile asked if I was copying out the Bible in longhand writing.

That casual remark hit me as a challenge and I decided there and then that I would copy out the entire Bible. I saw that such an exercise could be very useful in three ways – first, it would be an ideal way of learning and retaining the contents of the Bible, second, it would be good practice for writing, and thirdly, I would offer the finished book to the Save the Children Fund in the hope that they could auction it to raise funds for so many needy youngsters in the world.

I sat and pondered the task. It was obvious to me that it would take years of writing in my spare time, and I had precious little of that, to be able to finish the project. I was, perhaps, being just a little too ambitious. After some more thought I decided I would have a go at copying out the entire New Testament instead and bravely wrote "Page 1" on the first foolscap sheet.

I proceeded to copy from St. Matthew, Chapter 1 and wrote on both sides of the foolscap paper. On the second side, I had almost completed the page when I made a blot, and, tearing up the page, I started again. I had already promised myself that any error, blot or omission would not be amended, the page would have to be re-written because I wanted it to be a perfect copy.

Invariably mistakes occurred on the second page and both sides had to be re-written. It was laborious work but it taught me the Scriptures and to be extremely careful in my copy work.

For some days I enjoyed copying the New Testament as I had disciplined myself to writing for at least one hour every day. But by the time I had reached St. Luke, I was beginning to wish I had never started.

The task was proving to be far more time consuming than I had at first envisaged but, apart from this, the eye strain was considerable.

I looked at the pile of written sheets and considered there were too many to throw away, I looked at all the pages left to copy, and began to wonder if I would ever complete the task.

That very day I was led to read 2 Corinthians 12 : 9 "My grace is sufficient for thee," and knowing this to be true, I pressed on with new enthusiasm.

Seventeen months and 683 foolscap pages later the task was complete. It was a very happy day when I wrote, "The grace of our Lord Jesus Christ be with you all. Amen," and laid my pen down on the pile of papers which were now ready for binding.

The binder told me he had never bound anything like it before and made very favourable comments on the neatness of my handwriting. He also admired the four water-colour paintings of flowers which a lady friend of mine had done for this special copy. The paintings were the result of a real labour of love, since the painter had severe arthritis and found it extremely difficult to hold the paint brush.

It was another very happy day when I collected the finished work from the binder. The pages were securely bound in dark blue covers with the words "New Testament" printed in gold on the cover and the spine.

I looked at the bound Testament and wondered what I should do next. I didn't have to wait very long for the answer. Another colleague admired the manuscript and suggested I should write to famous people and request them to autograph it.

I instantly saw that this suggestion could serve a two-fold purpose. The famous signatures would make the New Testament quite unique and it was bound to enhance the sale of it on behalf of the Save the Children Fund.

I tentatively wrote to Dame Sybil Thorndike who was currently acting in a play at the New Theatre, Oxford, and received a very gracious reply in her own handwriting by return of post. I was warmly invited to meet her at the Theatre and she would be delighted to sign the Testament during my visit.

I found Dame Sybil even more charming than her note; she admired the book and encouraged me in the work. It was little wonder that I left the Theatre resolved to be more ambitious in my requests for autographs.

The response was quite overwhelming and periodically during the past eleven years I have been a guest of visiting foreign royalty, entertained at 10 Downing Street and the Houses of Parliament, not to mention a dozen Embassies and the top London hotels.

The Testament has taken me to premiers, princes, presidents and primates, from palaces to playhouses, from private estates to Parliament.

Seldom is a request turned down but often there are difficulties in meeting more than one celebrity in any one day. Either the appointments are so close together that it is impossible to keep both, or when one is in the capital, the other is absent. For this reason it has taken eleven years to collect one hundred signatures, bearing in mind the expense and time involved on each visit to London.

As I look at each signature I am reminded of an encounter or a special letter.

Through the writing of His Word and His special blessing, God has taken me to many famous people to speak for and about Him. As I have shared my Christian experiences with the famous, they in turn have shared their fears and feelings with me; but God has always been the centre of our conversation.

I cannot understand why a Prime Minister should ask for my opinion on a particular matter or why an Ambassador should seek advice. How is it that one who never got to grammar school should lecture at a University? My only answer to all of these things is that God is in control. He has used me, provided me with every tool to do His work, and gone before me preparing the way. The wonderful thing about Him is that He is able to equip all the way and no Christian worker need ever feel that He will let them down.

Did not Jesus say, "If ye shall ask anything in My name, I will do it." St. John 14 : 14.

Yes, this is my experience. As I have asked He has supplied and only a miracle working God could transform a non-writer to be a writer for Him and to use him as a witness to the famous in the land.

Would you seek to be used of God? His promise of St. Matthew 7 : 7 is for time and eternity. "Ask, and it shall be given you; seek, and ye shall find; knock, and it shall be opened unto you."

6

TO RUSSIA WITH LOVE

"GO TO RUSSIA!" The call from God came over very clearly.

Two years previously I had been privileged to attend a service in Birmingham conducted by a Rumanian Pastor who spoke of the way Christians were often persecuted for their faith in Communist countries.

I listened to his first-hand account of imprisonments, beatings and the hardships which fell upon Christian families. He and his wife had been in Communist prisons for years and had received tortures and suffered the utmost degradations.

Nothing less than a miracle secured their ultimate release and made it possible for them to come to the West. They were then currently engaged on a gospel preaching tour and sharing the plight of the persecuted Christians with all who attended the services.

The Pastor urged his congregation to pray for the church behind the Iron Curtain and I left the meeting with his words ringing in my ears. "The church situation in the Iron Curtain countries could prevail in Britain," he said, "it is already here like a baby tiger. When a tiger is small you can play with it, but one day the tiger will grow up and it can eat you. Pray for the persecuted Christians and pray for your own church."

I left the service with the resolve that I would pray daily for all Christians who were suffering persecution and torture. I didn't feel there was anything I could do physically but my faith rested in a God who answers prayers.

Two years later God answered those prayers in a way I least expected.

"Go to Russia," the call came again and again. I was praying for persecuted Christians world-wide but now in each prayer my thoughts were turning instinctively to the Christians in the Soviet Union. Although I did not quite know how to pray I was very much aware that God was trying to show me something. It was as though everything I touched or read screamed "Russia" at me.

Then two very strange things happened in a single week. A Christian printing organisation (with whom I had never had any previous contact and to this day I do not know how they got my address) wrote to say they had been able to print Bibles and New Testaments in the Russian language and requested prayer for the distribution of these Scriptures.

Secondly, the Area Youth Officer sent to me as the leader of a Mission Club, an envelope full of documents relevant to youth work, including details of a cultural exchange visit to Russia. There it was again – Russia – and now an invitation to apply for a visit to the country for almost a month's duration. But I read on and there were conditions; like representing the county (at that time prior to the boundary changes we were in Berkshire) and subject to permission being given for a month's absence from my place of employment.

I hardly thought it was worth applying. There didn't seem much chance of being accepted to represent the county, my little village gospel club seemed too insignificant in comparison with the large clubs of Windsor, Newbury, Reading and so on; and furthermore, I was in some doubt that my employers would approve of such a lengthy stay in an Iron Curtain country. Surely it would be foolish to apply and so I pushed the documents back into the envelope and proceeded to prepare a Sunday school lesson instead.

Out came my Bible for the lesson and I promptly received two jolts in quick succession. First from Isaiah 55 I read "For my thoughts are not your thoughts, neither are your ways my ways, saith the Lord," and then from 1 Corinthians, Chapter 1 "God hath chosen the foolish things of the world to confound the wise; and God hath chosen the weak things of the world to confound the things which are mighty."

That was it then, although it seemed to be foolish to apply for representation from such a small village club, God had just shown me in those two verses how He could undertake. Without any further hesitation I applied.

A series of miracles promptly followed the application. I was accepted for the trip to Russia and my employers were quite happy to grant permission for the leave of absence to visit a Communist country. The gospel printers sent along a free grant of Bibles and New Testaments in the Russian language and a sizeable money gift came in from a Christian supporter at the same time. The door was already open to Russia in answer to God's call but I still wasn't sure what He wanted me to do, apart from the fact He had supplied His word in Russian and it was obvious I had to take it in. But where did it have to go? I simply waited for the answer which had still not come when I left home and went off to join the tour party in London.

We travelled by train to Dover, boat to Ostend and then continued by train for an overnight stay in West Berlin. The following day we entered East Berlin and travelled to Schonefeld Airport and boarded a Russian jet bound for Moscow.

I was feeling decidedly uncomfortable when the plane landed at Moscow Airport in spite of spending most of the flight in prayer. I was hoping that my high nervous state was not showing as I was one of the first to leave the plane and walk to the waiting customs.

I firmly believe that walk was mightily used of God as He caused me to walk to the customs with a young man who was a radio broadcaster. Although we had been in the same party and travelled together for two days, the first time we ever conversed was between the plane and the Soviet customs.

The young man was carrying a tape recorder and explained that he wanted to record Russian music during the visit. It was his intention to play it on the radio when we got back to Britain. So the two of us entered the customs area together with the rest of the passengers following us.

Instantly the young man's tape recorder became the centre of attraction. All the customs officers came to it and wanted to know what was on the tapes.

The young man explained that the tapes were blank and he was taking them into the Soviet Union for recording music, but the officials were not satisfied. We all stood uncomfortably as tapes were played to prove they contained no recorded material.

All this time other planes were landing and more passengers joined the ever lengthening queue until a senior officer appeared and started to bark orders in Russian. It was obvious that the hold-up was causing confusion and the customs men were told to hurry up the proceedings. And hurry up they did! My case containing the Bibles and New Testaments was scribbled on along with a lot of others without so much as lifting the lid. I was still gasping with relief when minutes later we were on an Airport coach and speeding on our way to the Moscow Hotel.

During the Russian tour I discovered another active Christian in the party and we linked up and went on a search for a Baptist Church that we had heard about. We found it after some difficulty and stayed for the service, but, there was no God given indication that this was where God wanted the Scriptures deposited. The preacher admired the one and only Russian Bible I carried and gratefully accepted it when I offered it to him as a gift.

The days passed by and were full of official engagements in connection with the cultural visit. As I tramped around universities, art galleries and travelled extensively to be present at endless receptions, my thoughts often strayed to the cargo of Christian literature locked away in my case at the hotel. I asked myself, "Where did it have to go?" But the time was not yet ripe for the answer, and the travelling party moved on.

Soon it was apparent to me that God was at work. Due to some misunderstanding with a batch of official appointments, I found myself with a complete day free from any engagement.

As soon as breakfast was over I left the hotel with a single Russian Bible in my pocket. I knew that God had a special errand for me that day and by a very devious trick I managed to lose my Russian interpreter who insisted on never leaving my side.

For the first time I felt a sense of freedom and yet excitement as I wandered along a quiet road enjoying the sunshine. Then a bus came along and I knew I had to get on it.

I put the necessary kopecks for the fare in the appropriate machine and sat back for a trip I knew not where. It was fortunate that I did not have to state a destination since I discovered that a nominal fare charge is the same for a short or long distance.

I left the bus at a small town bus stop and just as I stood there wondering what I should do, another coach came along immediately, stopped, and the doors opened right where I was standing as a lone passenger.

Then I heard a voice, it was quite unmistakeable. "I have set before thee an open door, and no man can shut it." I saw the open door of this second coach was right at my feet and I felt myself drawn inside.

I popped my kopecks into the little machine and settled down for my second trip to an unknown destination.

This trip was longer than the last and I rode for about an hour and a half until I got to a railway station which was also the coach terminus. Since I was at a station I was beginning to think the next part of the journey was going to be by train. I still had no idea where I was going but I was absolutely confident that the Lord was leading me, and, step by step, the way was opening up before me.

I stood on the path where I had left the coach and another one came along and immediately, just as before, the doors opened at my feet and the words were repeated "I have set before thee an open door, and no man can shut it." This time I remembered the words were from God as found in Revelation, Chapter 3, because the following words came instantly to mind too, "for thou hast a little strength, and hast kept my word, and hast not denied my name."

And for the third time that day I went for a bus ride, which must have lasted another hour.

I was travelling through a very rural area now and saw workers, mainly women, working in the fields. Now and then the bus stopped to let a passenger off but no-one got on at all. It did not seem very long before I was the only passenger left on the bus and the driver kept staring at me. It was as though he sensed I was a foreigner and he did not want to speak to me. He still did not speak when we arrived at the terminus, he simply opened the doors and pointed for me to get off.

I stepped out into brilliant sunshine but I had no idea where I was. To the right of me I could see a small lake and to the left a sandy path which led up into a forest. In the distance, but still inside the forest, I could see the onion shaped dome of a church towering above the trees. My eyes then focused on a wide sandy path which led up into the trees, and in the sand I could see a mass of footprints.

In that instant I knew without any shadow of doubt that I was where God wanted me to be, and it seemed as though a command exploded in my brain, "Follow thou in my footsteps!" I did; I placed my feet in the footprints of the sand which led up into the trees.

The church was quite large and surrounded by a wide clearing within the trees, but to my very great surprise I found about 30 people, mostly elderly folk, sitting outside on rough benches. I observed that their faces seemed to shine, and unlike the other Russians I had met who never seemed to smile, these were smiling all the time. I just wandered among them and smiled and nodded to each in turn. They smiled and nodded back to me and then two gentlemen came up and one asked a single word question. "French?" "No," I replied, "I am from England!"

There was a silence for about a full minute before either of the gentlemen spoke again and I was conscious of all the other people staring at me.

Then the two gentlemen began to talk earnestly and indicated that I should sit beside them on one of the benches. A third man, very elderly, was called to us and more words were exchanged. I didn't know what was being said but it appeared that the third man was disagreeing with the other two. He suddenly left us to go into the church, muttering and shaking his head as he did so.

A few minutes later he emerged followed by a tall thin lady who must have been in her sixties or early seventies. She came straight up to me and smiled.

"You are from England?" she enquired in good English, "Why do you come here?"

"I am interested in the church," I replied.

"Why are you interested? Do you visit church in England?"

"I attend regularly, I am a Christian."

The lady then held a long conversation with the three gentlemen and the latter seemed to agree with all she said because they began to nod in unison.

At this point I pulled the Russian Bible from my pocket and offered it to her. The result was electrifying.

A murmur ran around the group of people sitting on the benches who, up until this time has remained completely silent and observed all that was taking place between the lady and the three men. Then they began to crowd round me and it seemed as though everyone began talking at once.

The lady silenced them all in an instant, then turning to me she said with some urgency in her tone "Come!"

I was not at all prepared for what happened next. Two men came up to me, one on either side, and taking an arm each I was led or rather frog-marched to a small door at the side of the church. I was taken down some stone steps and a small wooden door was opened as we approached. For a moment I thought I was being taken to a vault or a cellar.

I was ushered into a room which could not have measured more than 15′ × 12′ and all the people who were outside came in and packed the room. The gentlemen far out-numbered the ladies and I observed that the men sat on the chairs which were placed side by side all around the room, whilst the ladies, and some of the men, had to stand in the middle.

In one corner of the room was a small desk on which stood a very dim light but nothing else. Behind the desk an elderly man rose slowly to his feet from a very old chair. He was extremely tall and very reverently he took the Bible which the lady had handed to him.

The Bible was pressed to his chest by two hands and then he began to speak very quietly and slowly. This went on for three or four minutes and then all the men stood up and one by one stepped forward to kiss me.

I looked to the lady for some form of explanation and, seeing the look of puzzlement which crossed my face, she explained 1 Corinthians 16 : 20 "All the brethren greet you. Greet ye one another with an holy kiss."

The men sat again and all eyes were fixed on me. The man at the desk spoke again to the lady who in turn interpreted that they wanted me to speak to them.

"If you will speak slowly I will interpret for you," she said. I just said I was pleased to meet them all and that I was happy to know they were Christians. I then went on to say that I hoped the Bible would be useful.

At the mention of the Bible the drawer in the desk was opened and a copy, obviously owned by the Pastor who sat at the desk, was offered to me. I looked at this Bible and saw it was printed by the same printer and was identical in every way to the one I had brought.

"You are Roger's friend?" my interpreter asked, "We thank God for him and for sending you to us with the Bibles he promised!"

"I don't know a Roger," I began, and then out tumbled a most remarkable story.

Six weeks previously a young man by the name of Roger had arrived at this church with a very small quantity of Bibles. He had told these Christians that he thought he had found a way of getting the Bibles in and he would be sending a friend with a further supply in six weeks.

When I arrived the Russian believers thought I was Roger's friend and was bringing the Bibles he had promised. They were quite astonished when I said there was no connection, possibly but for mistaken identity, I may never have discovered this was part of the Russian Underground Church.

For the next hour I learnt much about the persecution of believers, how it was often impossible for them to get jobs and the brutal ways in which they were "dissuaded" from continuing to exercise their faith. They could not get Bibles and if these were found by the police they would be confiscated.

I learnt too that these believers met in secret in the little vestry vault beneath the church. The church itself was converted into a museum and the believers were all volunteers for cleaning and maintaining it as such. Although the authorities knew what was going on at the museum, they did not know what went on very regularly in the little room beneath it!

Converts joined the little fellowship which was steadily growing in numbers but they desperately needed more copies of the Scriptures for Christian study and growth. At last the reason for God sending me there was abundantly clear. I was meant to deliver those Bibles to these children of His.

The lady interpreter was then very swift to remind me of the lateness of the hour. When I gave her the district of my hotel she explained how I could return by a more direct route by taking two buses, and she did in fact travel a considerable part of the journey with me.

I was very careful to write down the details of the bus routes to the church area before I left and the times of two meetings in the week. It was quite clear that I would have to return in order to pass on the Bibles which I had just promised them.

When the lady left me at one of the bus stops I realised that three very great difficulties loomed up before me. How could I explain away the trick I had played on my official interpreter in losing him and explain my absence of several hours at the same time? Thirdly, with all the official engagements I had still to carry out, how could I arrange for another absence to coincide with one or the other of the next two church meetings? I knew that within a few days we would be moving more than a thousand miles away, so it was essential that I be present for one of the meetings.

I arrived at the final bus stop and found the hotel with no difficulty at all, and just as I expected the interpreter was sitting at a desk at the end of the corridor where my bedroom was situated. He was talking to a member of the hotel staff who sat at the desk to keep a security check on all the bedrooms.

I smiled as I went to the desk and asked for the key of my room.

"Where have you been?" he asked. "We have been very worried about you."

"I have seen a lot of countryside today," I replied. "I have taken five long bus rides and I have been to a museum." A lot more questions followed but he seemed satisfied that I had been on a sight-seeing tour, and he proceeded to tick me off in the nicest possible way for losing him earlier in the day.

I was not to disappear again, he was there to travel with me and he was in a position to show me the nicest places, he said.

I just smiled but did not trust myself to answer. I knew full well that another disappearance would have to be arranged in the next three or four days.

Official engagements prevented me from visiting the church for their next prayer meeting. Our party was taken many miles by coach for appointments which lasted right up until 9.30 that evening. As we returned to the hotel on the coach I was thinking about my new found Christian friends. No doubt they had been looking out for me and wondered what had happened to the precious Bibles they were expecting. One thing was certain, I just had to be available for the next service or my last opportunity of meeting them would be gone. We were due to move on the following day and here was a matter for real earnest prayer.

Well the Lord really answered my prayers and honoured His promise of Isaiah 65, "And it shall come to pass, that before they call, I will answer; and while they are yet speaking, I will hear."

The following day several of our party complained of stomach pains and headaches and voiced the opinion that we were being overworked on too full a programme. Some more relaxation was called for, and to my delight we had the option of attending the next day's engagements or taking a day of rest at the hotel. Our leader would just simply take smaller parties to the official functions and the ones that rested one day would be called upon to work the next and vice-versa. I was one of the first to ask for a day of rest which coincided with the day I needed to be free from engagements for visiting the church. My request was readily granted. I could see this was the Lord at work because through a chain of events it was the only free rest day I was given on the whole of the tour.

To complete my joy my interpreter was chosen to accompany the party on engagements and I was left alone in my room to write a report of the tour thus far.

I had a whole day free ahead of me, it was almost too good to be true and I didn't forget to thank God who I believe had made it all possible.

I prepared to leave for the church but my next anxiety concerned the case. How was I going to explain why I was carrying a case out of the hotel? And then the idea came to me.

Quite boldly and deliberately I humped my case down three flights of stairs and took it out into the garden. I sat with it in such a position that all could see I was using it as a low table for writing on. I sat and rested my pad on the case lid and scribbled my tour notes for about an hour. It got hotter as the sun climbed the sky and so I moved every now and then to a shadier spot. My thoughts were in turmoil as all the time I was getting myself nearer the gate. The whole process must have taken all of a couple of hours, since I felt a couple of students were paying me a lot of attention. I did not want to arouse suspicion by being too eager to get the case off the premises. I was finally positioned in a spot near the exit and when I thought the time was ripe, I casually stood up, popped my notes into the case, and strolled with it into the street and crossed the road.

I stifled the impulse to run but sighed a huge sigh of relief when I had put a couple of streets between the hotel and myself. My exit was not very timely, however, since I discovered I had almost two hours to wait for a bus. I found a small wall near the bus stop, popped my case behind it and sat on the wall and waited.

The service had begun when I arrived at the church and I found one elderly but very small man sitting on one of the benches that was perched precariously on the steps which led down to the cellar door. He smiled and beckoned for me to hurry forward.

When I got to the spot where he was sitting, the little man got off the bench and dragged it in such a fashion that two of its legs bumped from step to step. I was amazed to find this was a signal for someone inside to unlock and open the door.

As soon as the door was opened I was almost pushed by the little man to get inside as quickly as I could; then just as quickly the key was turned in the lock again and another man sat with his ear against the door.

The Pastor was speaking and motioned that I should sit beside him, and as I sat all the friends smiled and nodded, including the lady who had acted as my interpreter on the previous occasion.

Prayer followed and shortly afterwards the service ended.

A man in his twenties came straight up to me and shook me warmly by the hand. "You are most welcome," he said, "what has the Lord sent us, Christian brother?"

I took the Bibles, a few New Testaments and single page tracts from my case, and placed them neatly on the Pastor's desk, and without further ado he proceeded to pray. I couldn't understand a word but I felt he was thanking God for sending His Word.

I could see tears and the copies were very lovingly picked up and eagerly read. This proved to be a priceless gift to them and the Pastor directed their reading as they opened their new Bibles and found the special Scripture portions.

The joy was immeasurable but because of the shortage of buses in those remote parts I was not able to partake of it for long. As before the lady reminded me of the transport and prepared to undertake part of the journey with me again.

I was duly kissed again by all the members of the thirty odd congregation and I just wished I could have understood what they were saying to me. There were more tears of joy and they moved away in ones and twos, quickly and silently, to avoid any suspicion from outside.

The English speaking lady and gentleman were the last to leave with me and we left the Pastor sitting at his desk, reading his Bible by the dim light.

We walked back through the trees to the bus stop and I shall never forget the young man's words. "We thank God for these trees, they are our shade in summertime and shelter when it rains." Apparently it was not always possible to gather in the little room and on those occasions they fellowshipped under the trees.

The man left us at the bus stop insisting that I give Roger his Christian greetings when I see him. Then he gave a little bow and was gone.

The lady and I spoke about the Lord as we waited for the bus and she was clearly concerned about the atheism which exists in the land. She was so pleased to be able to share her faith with me and a great lump came up into my throat when she suddenly seized me by the shoulders. With tears streaming down her cheeks she said, "We pray for our brothers and sisters in the West. When you meet them, tell them we are praying for them and ask them to pray for us too."

So much did I enjoy this lady's fellowship it was as though I never wanted her to get off the bus. All too soon it was time for her to leave the vehicle and she waved until it turned a corner and was lost to sight.

Russian lady, tall, high colour, tear stained face, drab coat and little blue woollen hat, I never expect to see you again this side of heaven but I am carrying on your message. It is a good exchange – His Word to be matched with your unswerving faith, and may both work together to fulfil His command, "Go ye therefore, and teach all Nations, baptising them in the Name of the Father, and of the Son, and of the Holy Ghost: Teaching them to observe all things whatsoever I have commanded you: And, lo, I am with you alway, even unto the end of the World."

I was so thankful that the Lord was with me all the way. I often think about Roger, whoever he may be, and wonder if he was able to send that friend with the Bibles. Maybe it was not possible for him to go after all, so the Lord chose me, and every time I think of this I remember the words of Jesus, "Ye have not chosen me, but I have chosen you, and ordained you, that ye should go and bring forth fruit, and that your fruit should remain." Eternity will tell.

7

MEETING THE NEED

THE MAJORITY of the teenage boys and girls that come into my three Mission Youth Clubs wear St. Christopher medallions around their necks or have them hanging from key rings. Most of them travel into the villages where the Clubs are held on motor bikes, and St. Christopher is not only regarded as the preserver of travellers but no new bike ever appears without him.

"I've got a new bike, Ken," this is a regular topic of conversation, "and a new St. Christopher, do you like it?" I gaze on all shapes and sizes of the discs hanging on chains which range from brass to silver and even to gold. Some are very expensive but in the main the majority are not so.

The teenagers are quite serious about the presence of the disc and chain and ask such questions as, "He will look after me, won't he?" or, "I'll be kept safe if I wear this, won't I?"

Well I am quite frank and admit that I could never put my trust or assurance in a piece of metal, no matter who it represents or how expensive it is. Even so, many of the lads consider it to be sacred and would never dream of taking it off, even to wash, in the belief that to remove it from the neck is to remove the good fortune in safe travelling which it supposedly brings.

On the other hand I can, and have, put my trust in God, of Whom it is written in Psalm 121 "The Lord shall preserve thy going out and thy coming in from this time forth, and even for evermore."

In my ministry for the Lord I have found that He has preserved my travelling and kept me safe for several thousands of miles, but apart from this I have never bought a vehicle, as

He has sent along a motor cycle, a Ford Thames van, a minibus and a couple of cars. Thus I have proved St. Matthew 6 : 8 "Your Father knoweth what things ye have need of, before you ask Him," and Philippians 4 : 19, "My God shall supply all your need according to his riches in glory by Christ Jesus."

As I read these Scriptures I am conscious of one word which keeps recurring and that is "need." God does not promise to supply all that we want but He will give us that which is necessary to do His work.

My first experience of this came about 1963 when my only means of transport was a bicycle. I used it regularly to lead a weekly Mission Youth Club in a village some five or six miles away from my home. I carried all sorts of things on that old bicycle, including coal for the Youth Club fires, refreshments, books and a host of other things. Similarly I cycled to prayer meetings and took Sunday evening services as a local preacher as far as fifteen miles away. Often I was caught in thunder or snow storms, battled against heavy winds or suffered a multitude of punctures and other breakdowns, but I thoroughly enjoyed serving the Lord and took all these things in my stride.

Then I met an American service family who lived four miles from my home. In their early days in Britain this family went out to local churches to sing and preach and very soon I was invited to join them. Regular appointments for weekend preaching and singing were received and we met every Friday evening at the home which the U.S. Air Force had hired for the family because married quarters were not available at the base. At the Friday meetings we met for prayer and arranged the forthcoming programme of ministry, and soon we were travelling to many parts of the country under the title of the "Good News Gospel Team." Just as we felt the Lord had established us in this ministry a serious problem arose in that the U.S. Air Force ordered the family to move on to the military base. A married quarter had become available and the hired house was released.

It seemed that our essential Friday evening meetings for

prayer and programme arrangement would now have to cease. The move of the family to the base some eighteen miles away was too far to be reached on the bicycle and earnest prayer was made to find God's answer to the problem.

The day following the family announcement about the move, a friend and I joined a coach party outing to one of the Reading Youth for Christ meetings, and on the way home from this we stopped at a fish and chip shop for some refreshments.

A young man standing behind me in the fish and chip queue gently tapped me on the shoulder, and turning I found Mervyn from our coach party obviously wanting to have a word with me.

"Ken," he began, "as you know I am off to India soon to serve the Lord and there are several things I cannot take with me. I feel led of the Lord to give you my motor-bike, you do a lot of cycling for Him and it would be such a help to you."

I blinked back the tears which came to my eyes. Within twenty-four hours the Lord had answered my transport problem and I felt as though I wanted to cry with joy and gratitude.

A day or so later Mervyn arrived with the motor-bike and carefully explained how one went about riding it. I soon picked up the driving technique and the next Friday I was off to meet the American family armed with my Bible and a brand new copy of the Highway Code. How we praised the Lord that night for answered prayer and for supplying the need.

When I left the family at midnight my enthusiasm for the newly acquired motor-bike was literally dampened by a severe thunder storm. Undaunted, however, I tightened the helmet strap and set off for home.

Half an hour later I realised I was hopelessly lost. Going to the air base in daylight and the dry was one thing, now in the inky darkness and pouring rain it was another. The motor-bike lights didn't seem very bright and I knew I was going the wrong way. I thought I must have taken a wrong road out of the last town and now I realised I was really lost. The road I was on seemed endless and I didn't know whether to go on in the hope that I could pick up a new route for home, or turn back and go several miles back into the town and try and pick up the right road again from there. I just stopped at the roadside, ran my hand over the rain splattered headlamp and wondered what I should do.

"Are you lost?"

I blinked as a young man stepped out of a gateway and came across to where I was sitting on the bike.

"I certainly am," I replied and quickly explained my plight. "Well you are almost at Clanfield," the stranger went on, "turn round and go back into Bampton and take the Buckland road as far as the A420. You will easily find your way from there because it is well sign-posted."

It was really pouring now so I hurriedly thanked the stranger, turned the bike round in the middle of the road and headed back for Bampton.

Later when I got home and to bed I thanked the Lord for the motor-bike and for travelling mercies, and only then did the significance of that stranger at Clanfield hit me. Why did I stop at that particular spot? What was a man doing in a gateway at midnight on the lonely road? And in pouring rain too! As I thought more deeply about it I realised I did not see any transport, neither did the man appear to be wet as I was. My only explanation is that God must have had the right person at the right place at the right time. Could it have been my guardian angel?

I think of this every time I read Hebrews 13 : 2; "Be not forgetful to entertain strangers: for thereby some have entertained angels unawares."

The little motor-bike did me a very good service right up to the time the Americans were posted back to the United States. Then as one door closed, God opened up another by introducing me to a Christian family who were very faithful in keeping open a church which was struggling to maintain a congregation. The particular denomination decided to close the church in view of the very small congregation and the fact that the building needed urgent redecoration.

I admired the faithfulness and the zeal of this Christian family who worked tirelessly to keep the church open and maintain a witness to the village. To this end I offered my support and between us we decorated the church ourselves. In a wonderful way God provided a new coke stove in answer to prayer and all other needs were supplied too. It was a time of rejoicing and praising the Lord when the decision to close the church was rescinded.

From that time we have been very close friends and continually help each other in Christian service. By now the little motor-bike had come to the end of its very useful life and so I was back to cycling again, and loading the bike up with coal and goodies for the journeys to the Mission Youth Club.

Joyce, the daughter of the family which I had helped to redecorate the Chapel, had a car of her own and promptly offered to teach me to drive. The family was concerned with the way I cycled to the Club carrying such heavy loads and the fact that I got very wet when it rained. They decided that when I passed my driving test we would look to the Lord to supply a car, thus alleviating those two problems.

Joyce began teaching me to drive in earnest and before very long her patience was rewarded in seeing me pass the driving test; and then it was a case of praying for the transport.

God answered the prayer in the way we least expected. Joyce's parents had the offer of a vehicle which was not only a bargain but just the thing they needed, so they purchased it, and then offered me the old Ford Thames van they had been using hitherto. It came to me as a gift for the Lord's work and once again I was mobile for God.

The account of the blessings with the van would fill a book all of its own but a couple are worthy of a special mention.

A man by the name of Terry joined me with the Youth ministry and had a real desire to learn to drive. I could see that another driver would be an asset in the work and so I volunteered to teach him in the van.

It was a well known thing that whenever Terry and I went out in the vehicle, he always drove. We came to this understanding so that he would get maximum driving experience before going for his driving test.

During the period of instruction, a seventeen year old lad who shared my secular job was involved in a motor-cycle accident and died shortly afterwards from the injuries. We were not only shocked and heartbroken at this sad news the day we received it at the office, but a collection was made and I volunteered to visit the family that evening to convey our condolences and to deliver the gift.

The lad's home was about twenty five miles away and Terry, eager to drive as usual, offered to drive me on this sad visit.

We were travelling through the busiest part of Oxford when a sudden bang beneath the bonnet brought the van to a shuddering stop, and it was just impossible to get it going again.

The breakdown caused chaos within minutes as the traffic built up in the High Street, and I ran off to a nearby hotel to phone around for garage help. Half a dozen garages were either not interested in coming to our aid or did not have mechanics available to sort out the van.

I returned to the spot where it had broken down to find that some irate motorists had left their own cars and with Terry's help had pushed the van into a side road. One of these drivers was a mechanic from a well known garage, and having investigated the problem, had solemnly declared, "This thing has had it, you will never get that going again."

I was really anxious to visit the bereaved family of my young friend and I just did not want to accept this fatalistic pronouncement. I decided to telephone another garage and Terry went with me to a hotel for this purpose.

The reply was the same as before, shortage of mechanics and already overworked with emergency repairs. "Can you please come and look at it?" I begged, "I've just tried everybody and you're my last hope." I could see Terry staring at me and without any further word I put the receiver to rest. In that instant as I said "I've just tried everybody – " a voice spoke to my heart, "You have not tried me!" It just had to be the Lord!

In my haste I had run away from the van and made frantic telephone calls but not once had I thought of prayer, now I felt ashamed as Terry and I walked back to the vehicle.

The mechanic was still fiddling beneath the bonnet and muttered something as I put down the lid. "Well Terry," I said, "we will commit it to prayer. Lord, this is your vehicle and You know it is required tonight to undertake an errand for You. Will You be pleased to use it, and grant to us journeying mercies and we ask it in the Name of Jesus, Amen."

We got in and I turned on the ignition and instantly our little vehicle roared into life. The gear was engaged and we drove off to the absolute amazement of the mechanic who just stood and stared in bewilderment. And from that day I never did discover what the fatal problem was supposed to be because she just kept on running. God had evidently effected the cure and we gave Him all the glory for it. It is not surprising that in Genesis, Chapter 18 we read the words "Is any thing too hard for the Lord?" We certainly proved it wasn't that evening.

Terry kept up his regular driving lessons and continued to drive on every journey we went on together. I always insisted that he drove, not only for experience sake but for the fact we had applied for his driving test as well. He was very surprised, therefore, when one evening we had been out together and as we walked back to the car park to collect the van, I asked him for the keys and said I would drive us home.

"Why do you want to drive?" he asked, but I could not give any explanation. I just felt a compulsion to drive and took the wheel.

I was driving quite fast along a dual-carriageway between Oxford and Terry's home when something quite extraordinary happened. I felt a pressure on the top of my right hand which caused me to turn the steering wheel a good foot to the left. Consequently the van swerved and I mounted the bank at the side of the carriageway.

I started to apologise to Terry for giving him a fright when I heard a voice not more than three feet away from us.

"Thank goodness you stopped."

I opened the van door and there stood a youth with a motor-cycle and he appeared to be a little shaken. He explained that seconds earlier his motor-cycle lights had failed completely and had plunged him into total darkness. Had it not been for the pressure on my hand causing me to swerve, I would most certainly have mown the lad down and probably killed him because it was not possible to see him. But what caused me to swerve? I believe it was God at work again. David writing in Psalm 36 says of Him, "Thy righteousness is like the great mountains; thy judgements are a great deep: O Lord, Thou preservest man and beast."

It was not possible for the young man to repair the lights and as he was only a mile from home, we let him go on ahead of us and we lit up the way with our headlights, but I was rejoicing in the knowledge that the Greatest Light that shone forth that night was Jesus – The Light of the World.

Yes, the van was useful in so many ways and I never ceased to thank God for her. Terry had cause to rejoice too because she got him through his driving test at the first attempt. But as the van got older, the Mission Youth Club grew larger as problem teenagers poured into it. Some of the Club members were without transport so God provided me with the van for giving them a lift to it, and just at this time we had a lot of lads who lost driving licences too through drinking and driving offences. The number of young people requiring lifts grew each week until the little van was almost bursting at the seams. I knew that I was facing a crisis, I either had to refuse to pick up any more for the Mission Club or look to the Lord to supply a larger vehicle.

I never mentioned my transport problem to a living soul but

one weekend I made it a special matter for prayer. After all 1 Peter 5 : 7 says, "Casting all your care upon him; for he careth for you," and I did care for those teenagers and their need of transport to get to the Club.

Within one week of this special time of prayer for transport, I was led to visit some Christian friends of mine who supported the ministry. I really called at their farm to deliver a letter but my presence was more warmly received than the note.

"I hoped you would be calling in," said my friend, "I've got something to show you." Then he took me out into the farmyard and showed me a large twelve seater mini-bus in first class condition.

"That's yours to be used for the Lord," he said, and whilst I was almost speechless with this latest and sudden answer to prayer, he went on to explain the mechanics of the vehicle.

Now this fine Christian man did not know of my need for a larger vehicle and he certainly knew nothing of my secret prayer, but God knew, and He did the rest and supplied the mini-bus through His servant.

Jesus said in St. Matthew 6 "When thou prayest, enter into thy closet, and when thou hast shut thy door, pray to thy Father which is in secret; and thy Father which seeth in secret shall reward thee openly." And what an open reward the larger vehicle turned out to be. It is still used to convey all ages to services and Club meetings to this day.

The only drawback with a mini-bus, however, is that it can be too large a vehicle when there is only yourself or two or three passengers to convey to a Crusade or a meeting. I sometimes travel long distances to conduct meetings and the mini-bus was proving to be very costly on petrol, since it is not possible to do more than twenty miles to a gallon. What I really needed was the mini-bus for carrying large numbers of folk but a small car to get myself to meetings. I began to feel the burden of increased petrol prices so I increased my prayers and God went to work yet again.

Nigel, another helper in the ministry, owned a small Anglia

car which was in very good condition considering it was in its fifteenth year. The engine was extremely good and all was well with the car except a little welding and a few other jobs were required here and there. Sadly, but not more than Nigel expected, the car failed the Ministry of Transport test although, after prayer, I was convinced that the Lord was going to keep it in the ministry for a further year.

Nigel bought another car and offered me the chance of selling the Anglia as scrap metal, but I was still convinced that God had a use for it. I shared these thoughts with Nigel who gave me the option of doing what I liked with it.

A friend of mine, who undertakes welding and car repairs in his spare time, promised to do what he could on the Anglia and so I left it with him. Four days later he telephoned to say that he had not only completed the necessary welding on the car but it had passed the Ministry test too, so once again God had supplied the need!

The little Anglia car was used extensively in the ministry for the next couple of years. Then quite unexpectedly one evening, I was driving it home and was only two or three miles away when I felt a violent shuddering go through the car and I swerved for the bank.

In a flash I realised the steering had collapsed and there was nothing I could do to keep the vehicle under control. It mounted a bank, slid sidewards and I ended upside down in the bottom of a ditch with the car disintegrating around me.

I wriggled free as fast as I could, rejoicing and praising The Lord for escaping unhurt. I remembered the words of God in Exodus 33 : 14 "My Presence shall go with thee." It certainly had in this instance even to the bottom of a ditch.

I was soon to realise that I needed a replacement car if I was to keep the ministry going. I immediately cried unto the Lord and urged my Christian friends to do so too as I shared the news with them in a prayer letter.

A few days later the miracle happened. My telephone rang and, John, a Christian friend I had not seen for a year or two, was on the other end of the line. "Thank you for your recent prayer letter," he said, "we have been praying for you here in Liverpool."

I said how pleased I was with the assurance of prayer support and then John went on. "One of our Christian brothers here was present at our prayer meeting for you and went away with a burden on his heart concerning your loss of transport. This young brother, Paul, has since been led of the Lord to help you and I am to say he has decided to make you a gift of a car."

My eyes filled with tears when I thought of the Goodness of God and the obedience to Him of this dear brother in Christ whom I did not know. How he must love the Lord to make such a sacrifice that one of His servants should be kept mobile for Him!

Paul drove the car from Liverpool some days later and John and his wife drove their car too, in order to take Paul home again.

When I saw the Sunbeam Rapier in immaculate condition I was filled with joy and overflowing with thanksgiving. I hardly knew how to express my feelings to Paul for his love gift but I saw the pleasure in his face as he handed me the keys and invited me to get in. We went on a trial drive and Paul explained all the gadgets to me. It was all so wonderful and almost like a dream since I had never been in such a lovely car before.

I only met Paul that once but he is in my prayers regularly. I just know God will make it up to him in many blessings for a cup of cold water given in His name shall not lose its reward.

The same night that Paul delivered the car I dedicated it prayerfully to The Lord and His service. The very next day I had the joy of speaking to a young man in the car and had the thrill of leading him to Christ. I knew then that God's seal of approval was on the transaction.

A motor-cycle, the van, a mini-bus and two cars all supplied as a direct result of prayer. Not only does God supply the necessary transport to travel for Him but I have experienced

His blessings on the journeys as well.

Sometimes my friends are astounded when they see God's provision for me but I remind them that His provision is for them too as I share with them a portion of Psalm 37 "Delight thyself also in the Lord; and He shall give thee the desires of thine heart. Commit thy way unto the Lord; trust also in him; and he shall bring it to pass."

8

THE MASTER'S TOUCH

IF THERE IS a verse of all the Scriptures which appeals to me in a significant way it is St. Luke 21, verse 15 where Jesus says, "For I will give you a mouth and wisdom, which all your adversaries shall not be able to gainsay nor resist."

Bob, a friend of mine had been invited to speak at open air meetings at the little Oxfordshire village of Berinsfield. He was a powerful speaker, and I was very much looking forward to joining the party of Christians who went along to give him support.

A day or two before the meetings I developed a bad cold, a very sore throat and laryngitis; and when the day finally arrived I could only whisper and that was with difficulty. I had set my heart on going to the meetings, however, and turned up at the appointed pick up point to join the party in a dormobile.

The dormobile duly arrived but Bob did not. Several reasons, including a bad cold, kept him away and we left for Berinsfield in the hope that the friends there could provide another speaker at short notice.

As soon as Bob's absence was explained, our Berinsfield host turned to me and said, "Ken, since Bob has not come along today, we shall have to ask you to take the meetings for us!"

I pointed to my mouth and began to croak, "I cannot speak, I've got no voice."

"Well we shall just have to go to the bottom of our stairs," this friend said in such a matter of fact way, "and we shall ask the Lord to give you back your voice."

I tried to protest and vigorously shook my head, looking in an appealing way to the party in the hope that a volunteer would step forward and help me out of my dilemma. No-one moved but shot sympathetic glances in my direction.

"Come along Ken," our host was getting impatient now, "the best place to start is at the bottom of the stairs."

Slightly bewildered, and not just a little concerned, I followed the friend indoors where I was quickly introduced to his wife, then off into the hall we went and I was motioned to kneel on the bottom step of the stairs.

"This is my prayer spot," he explained, "we will just ask the Lord to anoint you by the Holy Spirit and empower you to speak for Him on this housing estate."

What a lovely prayer that man prayed. He thanked the Lord for the opportunity to speak for Him, thanked Him for sending me along in Bob's place, and then asked that I should be given the voice and words to speak. Finally he praised and thanked God for healing me and for granting the answers to his prayers.

But surely something was wrong. I did not feel one little bit healed, I was still whispering and my sore throat had not eased one little bit.

"Right, we'll have our first session at such and such a place," he went on, and we stepped outside to meet the party of friends who were waiting for us.

I coughed a couple of times and tried to put some volume in my voice between the house and the first spot assigned to hold the meetings, but my voice would not rise above a harsh whisper and attempting to make it so only made my throat feel worse.

We stopped at the side of the road and we were handed some hymn sheets. One of the young people in our party had brought along his guitar so singing started with musical accompaniment. It was quite impossible for me to sing and I began to edge my way over to a young man who was a gifted speaker. I was sure he would be happy to speak for God and help me out of a predicament at the same time.

And then a big lump seemed to come up into my throat and I thought I was going to choke. This led me on to a short fit of sneezing and suddenly I was able to breathe through my nose again.

I felt better instantly, and turning to the person standing next to me, I said, "This fresh air is helping me to breathe!" It was then I realised that the soreness and the whisper had disappeared. I was talking naturally again and all the pain was gone. This was more than what a breath of fresh air could do, this was a healing touch from the Lord!

Now I was being introduced and I stepped to the edge of the kerb to deliver the first gospel message.

I could see people standing in doorways and at open windows both upstairs and down as they listened to this Christian group. Several people were out in their gardens to watch us too but no-one actually joined our little party.

It was obvious that I should have to raise my voice if the folk at the windows and doorways were to hear me, so I drew a deep breath and began to shout.

What power there was in my voice that afternoon. I had left home with a painful whispering throat and now I was shouting at the top of my voice, and more than that, I was louder than at any time I could remember when I was really well.

I felt the Power of God surging through me as I delivered the gospel, then we moved on to the next meeting place and then the next.

It was as though the more I spoke the louder and better the voice became but this is typical of the miracle working of the Lord. When He performed His first miracle in Cana of Galilee by turning water into wine, the guests at the marriage found the more they drank the better the wine was – so it was with the healing of my voice, the more it was used for Him the better it got.

Wave after wave of power flooded me and more people were appearing in gardens to listen. I felt a real sense of the Presence of the Lord as His words were coming forth from my mouth, but all of a sudden those words of life were not favourably received.

A party of gypsy folk were living near the spot where I was speaking in the open air and as I stood at the side of the road speaking, one of them came along.

He was about a couple of inches short of six feet with long black very curly hair, about twenty-one years of age, muscular and as brown as a berry. He had a hard face, his hands were dug down in the pockets of some very ragged and faded jeans, and I could see one little gold ear-ring glistening in the sun.

As he drew near I noticed contempt written all over his face and his eyes swept me from head to foot.

"Why don't you go home, mate, and do a good day's work," he snarled, and like a bullet from a gun a reply shot forth from my lips. It was words given for the situation because I had neither thought, time to prepare an answer, nor, in those days, the courage to stand up to such a hard character.

"You talk of doing a good day's work, friend, but what is going to happen to you when your days of work are ended? What has eternity got to offer you?"

He swung round to face me, his face now looking murderous, and with fists clenched he marched across the road to meet me. A gasp went up from the little crowd of Christians standing behind me and I felt them drawing away. It was as though I was standing alone and the foe was preparing to knock me down.

I well remember that at that moment a surge of strength, such as I had never known before, went through my body. I was conscious of standing on the kerb at the side of the road to give me some height for speaking, but at this precise minute I felt very tall and in no way at all was I afraid of this awesome gypsy lad striding towards me. I was preparing myself for the onslaught when an amazing thing happened.

When he was within four feet of me he stopped suddenly as though he had hit an invisible barrier, his clenched fists dropped to his sides, his lips moved but no words came forth from them, but what struck me most of all was his eyes. Large brown eyes had been glaring at me, open wide and full of hate;

now as his fists dropped so did his eyes. He bowed his head, shrugged his shoulders and turning he slunk away without a word.

For a minute I thought he looked like a dog which had been beaten and was going away with its tail between its legs. Gone was the arrogance, the roughness, and I knew his toughness had been defeated. I wanted to say something more to the lad but the words would not come. I guessed God had had His own way of dealing with him regarding his days of work and his eternity.

I heard someone behind me say, "Praise the Lord," and we did together.

Later, going home in the dormobile, I thanked God not only for His Presence and Provision but for His Protection; and at the same time I thought on the words of Jesus which had become a reality in my own experience "For I will give you a mouth and wisdom, which all your adversaries shall not be able to gainsay or resist." And my emphatic reply to that is from Proverbs 30, "Every word of God is pure; He is a shield unto them that put their trust in Him."

9

HITCH HIKERS FOR HEAVEN

I SPOTTED HIM thumbing a lift long before he noticed me. It was pouring with rain and it was very late at night, and I was just leaving Reading en route for home. I had spent a very busy day conducting services in Surrey, now I was looking forward to getting home and to bed.

I slowed down to give the young fellow a lift. Ever since I received my first vehicle as a gift for the Lord's work, I promised Him that I would give a lift to anyone needing it. God had seen to it that I had transport and I wanted to share it with others on His behalf.

Whenever I give a lift to a hitch-hiker I am thrilled when the conversation eventually comes round to spiritual things. I put this down to one of three things, the hitch-hiker notices my sticker, "Smile, Jesus Loves You," on the dashboard, or the Scripture Union badge in my lapel, or more probably the Lord has directed our coming together. I believe God has His own way of revealing Himself to every human being in one way or another, and I look upon each lift as a Divine appointment.

From my first driving days I wanted some Christian literature to back up what I said in the car and to hand to the hitch-hiker as they left it. To this end I wrote a little tract called "Hitch Hikers for Heaven" which is published by the Evangelical Tract Society.

The blue and orange cover shows a young couple laden with cases waiting for a lift. The sign in the background points to "London," and it simply says:

HITCH-HIKERS FOR HEAVEN?

It was a pleasure to help by giving you a lift. I am even more happy to tell you of One who gave me a lift from the bondage of sin, and put me on the road which leads to eternal life.

A hitch-hiker is liable to miss the way and to be on the wrong road although he may think it is the right one; and the Bible says, There is a way which seemeth right unto a man, but the end thereof are the ways of death (Proverbs 14 : 12).

As a hitch-hiker you would not like to be taken down the wrong road, for such a route might well cause you to miss your destination. Likewise, you will not reach heaven unless you come the way of Jesus, for He said, I am the way, the truth, and the life (St. John 14 : 6).

There may be many roads leading to the place where you want to go, but there is only one way to heaven, for in the same verse the Lord Jesus said, No man cometh to the Father, but by Me.

Loaded down with travelling gear hampers the progress one could otherwise make, and carrying a load of sin by wrong living, turning one's back on God, immorality, drug-taking, alcoholism and so on, will surely weigh you down to such an extent that it will prevent your ever seeing the Kingdom of God, let alone entering it, unless the load is taken away. This is where Jesus meets the need.

Listen, friend. Christ said, Come unto Me, all ye that labour and are heavy laden, and I will give you rest. Take My yoke upon you, and learn of Me; for I am meek and lowly in heart: and ye shall find rest for your souls. For My yoke is easy, and My burden is light (St. Matthew 11 : 28–30).

Yes, burdens can be lifted since Jesus Christ bore our sins in His own body on the tree (1 Peter 2 : 24). He took the weight and guilt of our many sins, even the worst of them, when He died at Calvary. Just as you accepted the lift the Lord Jesus invites you to accept the benefits that are available to you as a result of what He has done in suffering and dying for you on the Cross. Will you ask Him to forgive you, and cleanse you from your sins today, and then, simply trust Him to come into your life and remain with you for ever?

You see, when they put the Saviour to death that was not the end of Him, for He rose from the dead on the third day. It is Christ that died, yea rather, that is risen again, Who is even at the right hand of God, Who also maketh intercession for us (Romans 8 : 34). It is not a dead Christ I am offering you, but One who is alive today!

As many as received Him, to them gave He power to become the sons of God, even to them that believe on His Name (St. John 1 : 12).

Remember, you can't thumb your way to heaven, but Jesus can ensure you get there if you will go His way. Make sure you are on the right road today.

In the past four years I have given lifts to hundreds of hitch-hikers and consequently given away hundreds of these little tracts. I call this part of the ministry "Mission to Hitch-Hikers" and I encourage other Christians with cars to prayerfully consider serving the Lord in this way too. I have found many opportunities to speak for God in this way and much blessing has come as a result of it.

Now coming out of Reading in the pouring rain, this small, thin young fellow was thumbing a lift. He had no raincoat and the trousers and pullover which he wore were looking quite wet.

"Thanks a lot," he said as he climbed into the car, "I would be grateful for a lift as far as Newbury if you're going that way."

I knew immediately that we wanted different roads, he required the A4 whilst I needed the A329, but I felt a sort of a compulsion to go out of my way for his sake.

He was very pleasant and talked a lot so that it was difficult for me to say a word. I listened to his explanation as to why he was without his own car that night, heard how he had missed some public transport, and learnt that he was fearful of missing his connecting bus from Newbury due to the lateness of the hour. It was only then that I discovered he was a jockey of talent and reputation and that he was on his way home.

"What have you been doing today?" he asked and I told him about the services where I had been preaching and this opened up a discussion on Christian things as we drove on through the rain.

It was not long before I discovered this young man was very unhappy and burdened with a lot of personal problems. It was as though ht was bursting to share these with someone and out tumbled his story.

"I have not been married very long," he began, "and my wife is expecting a baby. She is not very well so I have taken her to her mother's home and I have left her there for a while to get better."

I sympathised and asked the young fellow if the absence of his wife meant that he would be looking after himself for a while.

"Yes," he replied, "and unfortunately it might be for a long time."

"Until after the baby is born?" I enquired, but he shook his head.

"No it's more difficult than that," he went on, "you see being a jockey takes me to live in isolated places where the horses train, and my wife is used to the town. Where we are living now is deep in the country and she cannot stand the loneliness, especially when I'm away racing. She misses her folks and the shops and all in all she seems to be on the verge of a nervous breakdown."

I detected a catch in the man's voice and for a moment or two I thought that he was going to break down in a flood of tears.

"My biggest problem is making up my mind whether or not I should give up my career," he said and went on to explain. "As I see it a jockey's life is spent mainly in the country and my wife just cannot take it. I don't want to lose her and the baby when it comes but racing is my life too."

I had to admit this man had a problem and I confessed that if I was in a similar situation I would pray for the answer to it.

The conversation then turned to the jockey's career and I found his account of racing life quite fascinating, so much so that I volunteered to drive him to his home. It was not far away by this time and it was obvious that he had missed the last bus to the nearest stop to his home, and it was still raining anyway.

He was right about living in an isolated spot for he directed me round twists and turns in a road which was only wide enough to take one car; but very soon we had arrived outside his house.

"Please come in and have some coffee," he invited, but I looked at my watch and saw it was now very late. I hesitated.

"I would be pleased for you to come in," he insisted, "and I'll show you my racing awards."

It was just as though he did not want to go into that empty house alone and I could feel his loneliness, so we went in together.

As we waited for the milk to boil, my jockey friend fed the budgerigar and took me into a room to show me his racing awards. I had never seen such magnificent trophies and I was thrilled to hear how each was won. I could now understand more fully why this young man was keen to go on in his racing career.

Apart from being a first-class jockey I discovered he was a very talented painter too, and once he had made the coffee, he showed me some of his paintings. It was not surprising that most of them were of horses, they played such a big part in his life.

Here was a man who had almost everything that fame and fortune could give him, but he lacked peace and was of all men most miserable. We talked a great deal more and then he accepted the hitch-hikers tract and my prayer with a whole lot of gratitude. Later he waved me off into the rainy night and I knew he was a lot happier than when I had picked him up a couple of hours earlier, and, with prayer he can find the words from the tract a blessing in his own experience. Jesus said "Take my yoke upon you, and learn of Me; for I am meek and lowly in heart: and ye shall find rest for your souls. For my yoke is easy, and My burden is light."

Rainy nights seem to be a good setting for picking up talented folk for it was such a night when we picked up a young actor.

Co-workers Joyce and Nigel had joined me on a trip to Faringdon where a gospel meeting for teenagers had been arranged at a public hall. We had prepared a pile of food and took along bottles of lemonade and waited for the young people to turn up. But in spite of a lot of advertising, not a single soul came to the meeting. This was an unusual occurrence for Faringdon and we just could not understand it. What were we going to do with all the food which had been prepared? Then I had an idea, we would go to a home near Swindon where a family held young people's meetings and we would off-load all the food there for the hungry youngsters.

The food was duly delivered but we did not stay very long and Nigel started to drive us home in my minibus in the rain. We had only gone a mile when we saw a young man thumbing a lift at some crossroads. I instinctively reached for a tract as Nigel stopped to pick him up.

"You will not have heard of the little place where I am going," he said and named a village only five miles away from where I live.

"If you don't mind going a bit off the route so that the driver can drive himself home," I replied, "I will be able to drop you at your home afterwards." He was very pleased about this because it was an extremely dark and wet night and he lived way across country. It would have been almost impossible for him to have got a direct lift and he was very grateful at the prospect of getting home in the dry. Nigel dropped Joyce at her home and then drove himself to his own where I took the wheel. As the hitch-hiker and I travelled the next few miles together he had suddenly become very quiet as though going home had something sinister about it.

Then I surprised myself with the statement which came forth

from my lips, although I should not have been surprised because I have experienced this power over my tongue before.

"You cannot run away from your problems," I said, and he swung round to face me.

"How did you know I was running away?" he asked, but I just shrugged because naturally I had no idea that he was running away.

"I just know you have problems," I continued, "and I don't believe it is pure coincidence that I picked you up tonight." I went on to explain the strange circumstances which had brought us together. If the youngsters had turned up at the Faringdon meeting we would not have been on that road at all. Did God intend them not to be there but had other work for me to do with this young fellow instead?"

At this time we arrived at the man's home which was in total darkness but he indicated that he wanted me to stop and talk to him in the drive, so we sat in the minibus and chatted.

"My wife and I have had problems," he explained, "and after a row today I just decided to run away. For some unaccountable reason I just could not take any more. I did not know where I was running to, I simply decided to walk up to the main road and go as far as the first car would take me."

"And the first lift was not travelling very far?" I asked, but he interjected.

"On the contrary, the driver said he was going as far as Bristol and I told him that was where I wanted to go too. He drove me about twenty miles, well to the spot where you picked me up, and I suddenly had this urge to leave the car. I asked him to drop me there and with some surprise he did so. I believe he thought I was mad!"

So that was it, now I was thinking our meeting was not mere coincidence after all.

The young man began again, "At those crossroads I suddenly felt that I should come home again and I could not believe my luck when your friend stopped to give me a lift. And then when you said you could bring me right home it seemed too good to be true." He was thoughtful for a moment or two and then asked a single question.

"Do you mind if I smoke?"

I agreed and he lit a cigarette. The moment I saw his face by the light of the match I knew I had seen it before and I said so.

"You have probably seen me on television," he said and then gave me his name: and I was happy to become better acquainted with this young talented actor. For the next few minutes we discussed his career and I was pleased to see him becoming more relaxed, and then he went on to explain his personal problems in depth.

Some time later he invited me in for coffee but I declined because I had no wish to disturb his wife at such a late hour. I reasoned that as they had left each other on strained terms it might be far better for them to make it up in private; and he was willing for us to pray together on this very matter.

I left then but not before I had assured him that I would return at some other time and promised to meet his wife.

A few days went by before I called at the home again and meeting the young actor and his beautiful wife was a rich experience. We spent a very happy evening together and became good friends. My prayers had been answered in a wonderful way, the family was reconciled and there was real evidence of love. I was so glad of that meeting at the crossroads.

The weeks slipped by and our friendship grew, and one of my happiest memories is the evening we spent at a play together. After the play we went out to dinner in a place where a small orchestra was playing. As we dined the leader of the orchestra announced that he had some congratulations to hand out and a special piece of music to play, then he congratulated me on the publication of my book "Road to Nowhere". I was astounded until I saw the actor grinning at me, it was he who had tipped the orchestra off. I watched the couple over dinner and saw the love they had for each other, and in this instance I rejoiced that God had had His way over

Bristol.

I have found hitch-hikers thumbing lifts all over the country for one reason or another and many of them have interesting stories to tell. The saddest, however, concerns poor old Joe.

Meeting Joe was an unforgettable experience. It was a moonlight night and a sharp frost glistened on the ground. Although well wrapped up in a thick overcoat I still felt the cold as I drove along a lonely road in the minibus. My hot breath was causing vapour and I was finding it increasingly difficult to see where I was driving because of the build up of ice on the windscreen.

All of a sudden I spotted an elderly gentleman shuffling towards me, he was wearing an old Army overcoat and a cap and stopped every now and then to blow on his hands.

For a minute I wished he had been travelling in my direction so that I could have given him a lift, he looked so pathetic, obviously very down at heel, and extremely cold.

He stopped and looked as I drove by and I could see him still watching as I glanced in the mirror.

"You are like the priest who passed by on the other side in the story of the Good Samaritan," I thought, "it wouldn't be much out of your way to turn back and offer some help on such a cold night."

I turned in the next gateway and went back to the spot where I had first seen the old man. He was still standing there and his unshaven face looked grey and wet in the moonlight.

His old Army overcoat was supported at the middle with string and I could see some old socks were acting as gloves on his hands. He had a dreadful smell about him and he swayed from foot to foot in old thick and heavy looking boots.

"Would you like a lift?" I asked but he stared at me in silence. I tried again. "Are you going to Oxford?" "Not tonight its too far," he wheezed, "I shall find some trees presently and go on in the morning."

"Surely you are not staying out all night in this cold, are you?" I enquired but he fell into silence again.

I didn't like the sound of his breathing and he was constantly wiping his nose on his be-stockinged hand. He still shuffled from one foot to the other and I imagined that his feet must be very cold, nigh on frost bitten I shouldn't wonder!

"Come on get in the minibus," I urged, "I'll drive you into Oxford, I cannot leave you to stay out here all night."

I climbed back in the minibus and waited for him to get in the passenger side, but I soon found it was not possible for him to do so. It appeared that he was almost numb with the cold and I had to lift him in.

I had no idea where I could take the man, and then I remembered the centrally-heated Chapel schoolroom which I had just left. I had just come from leading the village Mission Youth Club and the room would still be warm. I could make him a hot cup of coffee there and give him something to eat whilst I decided what I could do with him.

On arrival at the Chapel schoolroom I made the man comfortable and put the kettle on to boil. He told me his name was Joe and his home had been in Ireland. As far as he knew all his relatives were dead and he just travelled the country doing odd jobs here and there.

Joe gratefully accepted the coffee and drank it down in noisy slurps, warming his hands around the cup as he did so.

Every sentence he uttered was punctuated with a "sir" and I was a little taken aback when he said, "Could you do something for my feet, sir?"

I knelt down beside him and started to untie the laces of his ancient boots. The stench was awful and I had a hard job to free his feet from the things and then to my horror I discovered his very ragged socks were oozing with blood.

I gently peeled the socks off and lifted his old grey trouser legs and the sight which met my eyes made me feel quite sick. Ulcerated legs and raw feet were seeping with wet matter and blood and I felt sure that gangrene must be there because of the foul smell. I know that nothing but the Grace of God helped me in this dreadful situation.

As Joe nibbled biscuits I prepared a bowl of hot disinfected water and began to clean the dirt off the open wounds. Every minute the smell seemed to get worse and I hated what I was doing, but one look at the old man's face peering down into mine reminded me that he needed urgent treatment.

There were places on his shins where the flesh had been eaten away almost to the bone and his toes were almost skinless too, and several toe nails were in-grown.

It took some time to clean up all the raw places and then I had to look round for some bandaging. I had to make do by tearing up a clean towel and wrapping the pieces around his legs and I held them in place by loose elastic bands because I did not have any safety pins.

I told Joe I just had to take him into Oxford where he could get the necessary treatment.

Joe was already feeling very much better and some colour was returning to his grey lined cheeks. "This is a church isn't it sir?" he asked, "I believe in God you know, do you think you could loan me a Bible, sir?" I was very happy to give him one out of the cupboard and then I insisted on getting him into care in Oxford.

On the journey poor Joe kept thanking me for the Bible, it was as though it had become a personal treasure to him and was much more important than the treatment on his legs and feet. His last words to me as I left him in good care were, "Thanks again for the Bible sir, I shall read it and look after it," and I prayed for the Lord to look after him too.

Joe's appreciation for the gift of the Bible is equalled only by that of Neil's, another hitch-hiker who I picked up very late one Sunday evening. It was not a case of handing Neil a tract when He left the car because he saw it under the dashboard almost as soon as he got in and he asked if he could read it.

"Are you a Christian?" he asked and I replied that I was.

"What's your definition of being a Christian?" he pressed, and I told him that it means being a "Christ's One" or more simply one that belongs to Jesus Christ.

"But surely we all belong to Him?" he persisted but I pointed out that the Bible has something very important to say on that point. I referred him to Romans Chapter 8 "Now if any man have not the Spirit of Christ, he is none of His."

This came as a jolt to Neil and he started to ask searching questions regarding Scriptures as we drove along.

Neil turned out to be an undergraduate at Oxford University and he started to criticise the Bible from an intellectual point of view. I said he reminded me of Nicodemus to whom Jesus said, "Art thou a master of Israel and knowest not these things?" and he laughed good naturedly and said, "Well go on then, tell me what Jesus Christ has done for you!"

I was glad of the opportunity to tell Neil how Christ had shown me many miracles in my life. I had seen Him at work in many wonderful ways but my faith was centred on the fact that He loved me so much that He was willing to die for me on a Cross at Calvary. By faith I accepted that Christ had died in my place, once and for all for my sins, and the shedding of His Blood was to wash away those sins. That was why it was necessary for Christ to come to this earth, for it was written there in the tract where He said, "I am the way, the truth, and the life: no man cometh unto the Father, but by Me."

It had suddenly become very clear to me that unless I let Christ deal with my sins I could never enter into Heaven because in Romans 6 it says, "For the wages of sin is death; but the gift of God is eternal life through Jesus Christ our Lord."

"You have to accept a gift," I explained, "and it is necessary to accept God's gift of forgiveness for sin in the Person of Jesus Christ His Son; there again it says "But as many as received Him, to them gave He power to become the Sons of God, even to them that believe on His name," and in the third Chapter it is qualified by the words, "For God so loved the world, that He gave His only begotten Son, that whosoever believeth in Him should not perish, but have everlasting life."

"I have accepted the salvation which Christ died to give me," I went on, "and since I now serve One who rose from the dead I know power and purpose in my life and that is why I have gone out to preach about it today."

"I see I need to accept Christ," Neil said thoughtfully and quietly, "but how do you do it?"

"You need to ask for it, to pray for it," I explained, Jesus said, "Ask, and it shall be given you; seek, and ye shall find; knock, and it shall be opened unto you: For every one that asketh, receiveth; and he that seeketh, findeth; and to him that knocketh, it shall be opened."

"I don't think I'm good enough to be a Christian really," sighed Neil, "but I would like to be one."

"Well the Bible answers your statement," I said, "in Romans 3 it declares, "There is none righteous, no, not one," but in the third Chapter of Revelation Christ still promises, "Behold, I stand at the door, and knock: if any man hear my voice, and open the door, I will come in to him and will sup with him, and he with me." "It's up to you now, Neil, if you have heard Christ speaking to you tonight you can open up the door of your heart and give Him a place in your life. I know you will never regret it because He is a rewarder of them that diligently seek Him." I then told him about my Mission Youth Clubs for problem teenagers and explained how several of them, of his own age group, had swopped their problems for Christ by placing their trust in Him.

Now we were coming up to the roundabout where Neil wished to leave the car and for the first time I noticed it had stopped raining and a watery moon was shedding more light.

"I'm really grateful to you for speaking to me about your faith," he said, "and when I get back to college I am going to read this tract again and pray. I'm really glad I met you because I feel God wanted me to know about Him."

Neil was out of the car now and was standing with the door open. He thrust his hands deep into the pockets of his jeans and withdrew some coins and hastily counted them.

"Will you please accept this?" he asked, "I'm afraid its only 58p but its all I've got and its worth it for what you've told me tonight."

"Please hang on to it," I said, "I'm sure the Lord will give you a use for it."

"You are welcome to it to help your Mission Club," he insisted and I was touched by the sincerity of his offer. Although I insisted that Neil should keep the money to meet some of his own needs, I recognised that in his estimation the knowledge of salvation was worth all he had. Then as we shook hands and he walked away I was convinced that Neil had become rich in the sonship of Christ.

A lift, a gospel tract, a word in season, all these are simple things and yet all work together to make God known, and He shall have the final word and glory for it. "So shall My word be that goeth forth out of my mouth: it shall not return to me void, but it shall accomplish that which I please, and it shall prosper in the thing whereto I sent it."

10

CRUMBLING FOUNDATIONS

"CAN YOU COME quick Ken? Mervyn is lying in the toilet and I think he's unconscious!" The boy was no older than 13 and his flushed face looked up at mine with pleading in his eyes.

I was at the Youth Club making coffee when the lad burst into the kitchen, so I promptly dropped the jar and ran round to the outside toilet.

Mervyn is only twelve years old and I certainly didn't expect to find him in the state he was in. I found him lying on the toilet floor, face down in his own vomit.

"Mervyn," I called as I gently rolled him over on his side, but his small body was convulsive with retching and a strange sound was coming from his throat. He was very cold and his closed eyelids fluttered as I called his name for the second time.

The smell of alcohol was almost overpowering and it was then I realised he was blind drunk.

"He's been drinking," said his young friend as if in answer to my thought, "better take him home hadn't we?"

At that minute an older boy came into the toilet, "Is he drunk again?" he asked, "you want to leave him there, mate, and let him die."

That was the last thing I wanted to do and I made up my mind that I would get him home as fast as I could. There was a crowd of youngsters at the Youth Club that night and it wasn't wise to leave them unsupervised for long.

I had no idea where Mervyn lived and I was wondering what his parents were going to say when I got him home in that state.

"I'm Bill, his best friend," the other lad chirped up again,

"I'll come with you and show you where he lives if you will put him in your minibus."

I tried to lift Mervyn on to his feet but it was impossible for him to stand and he slumped to the floor once more. He was a deathly white and his lips were blue and his eyes were rolling uncontrollably. I had no alternative but to pick him up and carry him to the minibus.

The boy was small for his age and was wearing part of a school uniform which was ruined; his grey pullover was covered in sick which stuck to me as I carried him to the vehicle, and I felt both cross and yet sorry as I sat him upright on the wide seat at the front of the minibus.

Bill sat beside his friend and put an arm around him and was muttering sympathies as we drove away from the Youth Club, and he stopped every now and then to tell me the way.

It seemed as though Bill was conversant with Mervyn's life style so I began to quiz him. "Where did he get all that drink?" I asked.

"Down the pub," was the quick reply.

"They wouldn't serve him with alcohol," I replied, "you can see he is no older than 12."

"He stands outside and the older ones bring it out to him," Bill went on, "he cadges drinks off everybody."

During that journey to Mervyn's home I discovered that other boys from the Youth Club were buying alcohol at the pub and passing it on to younger friends outside. Now I was concerned, not only that the younger members were receiving the drink but the lads who were actually buying it were as much as two years too young to be able to buy it within the law. It must be very difficult for landlords to be able to assess the ages of some of these youngsters, so many of them are tall and mature for their age, especially the girls; even so, I am convinced that in many instances the landlords do know they are selling alcohol to customers who are under age, but they turn a blind eye because its good for trade.

It is sad but true that you very seldom see a policeman in a village and in small communities where everyone knows everyone else, bar staff are bound to know the youngsters and whether or not they are still at school or out working.

Soon we arrived at Mervyn's home which was a newish council house on a small estate. The house was in darkness and Bill broke into my thoughts as to what I should say to the parents.

"You bring him in and I'll get the key," he said. My spirits sank to zero as only then I realised the parents were not at home. What was I to do? I couldn't take him back to the Youth Club in that state and I was getting more anxious that the Club was still without supervision. I needed to be in two places at the same time. Here is a typical situation where another Christian helper would be so welcome, and, circumstances which Jesus Himself describes in St. Luke 10, "The harvest truly is great, but the labourers are few: pray ye therefore the Lord of the harvest, that He would send forth labourers into His harvest."

Bill had apparently taken Mervyn home on several occasions and knew where the family hid the key to the front door. He found it, opened the door and went in and switched on the light.

Mervyn started to mumble some sort of incoherent protest as I picked him up and carried him to the house.

"Put him on the sofa," Bill commanded and I sat him there. Bill then went off to the kitchen and returned with a bowl which he placed at Mervyn's feet.

"There's the bowl if you want to be sick again Merv," he said, and I had a feeling that this lad had done this before, everything came so naturally to him.

I looked at Mervyn who kept falling flat on the sofa, he looked extremely ill and I didn't feel as though I could leave him. I sat him upright but everytime I took my hand from his arm he fell flat again.

"Have you any idea where his parents are?" I asked Bill, but he shook his head.

"They go out to different pubs," he said, "when they get

home they will be worse than he is; they will not even know he's drunk."

I tried to find out from Bill if there were any other relatives near, I felt a responsibility to Mervyn since if I left him in that state and anything happened to him, I would not be held blameless.

"He's got an elder brother down at the Youth Club," Bill explained and described a very tall lad who had recently joined us. I had not connected these two as brothers before.

I assured myself that Mervyn was in no immediate danger and made him comfortable on the sofa before I left. It was then a quick return to the Youth Club where I singled out the brother cuddling a girl in the corner.

I quickly explained Mervyn's plight to the brother and endeavoured to press my point with emphasis. "When I was in the R.A.F.," I said, "a senior N.C.O. was drunk one night and returned in a similar state to his quarters, next morning he was found to be dead having choked himself with his own vomit. I don't want this to happen to Mervyn, will you please go home and stay with him?"

"Let him die then if he's got no more sense than to get in that state," the brother sneered, and I felt very sad because this was the second time that night I had been told to let him die. Who cares for the Mervyns of this world? And the brother was more concerned to turn to the girl friend and start kissing all over gain.

"I'll take you back home in the minibus," I insisted and poked the brother not too gently between the shoulder blades. He could tell I was more in earnest now and as I promised to be a continuing threat and interruption to the matters he currently had on hand, he swore, muttered, and pulling the girl friend by the hand said, "Come on then, let's get it over with!"

I made my second trip to the home and went in with this young couple to see how Mervyn was. He sat just as I left him, staring at the patterned wallpaper at the far side of the room, the bowl, thankfully still empty, at his feet.

The brother swore again and kicked Mervyn's foot, then he dragged him off the sofa and dropped him into one of the easy chairs. He then threw himself on the sofa and patted the cushion beside him indicating that the girl friend should sit there.

"Well I must get back to the Club," I said, "you will be all right now, and I don't want you to leave young Mervyn."

"Put on the telly," was the brother's only reply but I ignored it and with a simple "Good-night" I let myself out.

Billy was still in the minibus and he chatted incessantly as I drove back to the Club. "You don't want to worry about Merv," he breezed, "he's like that every week and he will be better tomorrow. It don't do him no harm, anyway his old man and woman are just the same!"

I prayed a lot for Mervyn that night as Billy's words kept coming back to me: "His old man and woman are just the same," and I prayed for them and their influence on this young life too.

The more I pray for these problem youngsters it seems the more I am led to think of the Commandments and where God declared He would visit the iniquity of the fathers upon the children unto the third and fourth generation. Therefore, great responsibility falls upon parents and it behoves them to heed the Word of God as it is found in Proverbs 22, "Train up a child in the way he should go: and when he is old, he will not depart from it."

Jeffrey was another pathetic little chap. I found him leaning against the wall of the Chapel schoolroom one evening whilst the Mission Youth Club was going on inside. I estimated he was nine or ten years old.

"Can I come into the Club?" he asked as I popped outside to put something in the car.

"You are too young for the Youth Club," I explained, "we do not take boys and girls under 13 but you are very welcome to the Good News Club for juniors on Sunday at 2.15 p.m."

"Go on let us in," he pleaded but I had to say we must abide by the rules. If I let one youngster in they would all want to come and chaos would be the result.

A sharp white frost lay thick and glistening on the ground and it was one of the coldest nights of the winter. Jeffery huddled up against the wall, shivering, which wasn't surprising since he was only wearing some very old jeans, and a pullover that was full of holes, and daps.

"Why don't you go home," I encouraged, "you will get frozen there," and muttering he started to walk away.

Half an hour later I stepped outside again, this time to put something in the dustbin. To my surprise the lad was still standing against the wall with his hands, which by now were almost blue with the cold, wrapped around his arms. "Go on, mister, let us in," he pleaded again and I noticed he was shaking like a leaf.

"Good gracious!" I exclaimed, "what are you doing here still? You must be frozen, why don't you go home?"

"I'm afraid," was his sad reply.

"Afraid, what are you afraid of?"

It was obvious that he was trying to evade my question. "My big brother is in there," he continued, nodding in the direction of the Youth Club, "can I come in and stay with him?"

I asked him who his brother was and then asked him again why he was afraid to go home. "Are you in any trouble?" I asked.

"No, there's nobody in and I don't like staying there on my own."

"Where are your parents then?"

"They've gone to a party," he said and named a well known pub in the area.

It was clear to see that Jeffery was abandoned, he was too frightened to stay at home alone and he had nowhere at all to go. I could understand his coming to the Youth Club where the chance of warmth and company was inviting and he felt a sense of security in the presence of big brother.

Without any further hesitation I invited him in and made

him a scalding cup of coffee. He just cupped his hands around the cup to warm himself and took a long time to drink it. It also took him a long time to stop shivering.

I was pleased to see that the older brother took a lot of interest in Jeffery and encouraged him to play draughts with him. These two obviously got on very well together and at closing time they left promptly with the big one's hand on the little one's shoulder. I watched them go off into the freezing night, chatting and laughing noisily.

I imagined the parents at the party and guessed they were not giving these boys a single thought; somehow it made the Mission Youth Club all that more important. It was a place where they could learn of a loving Heavenly Father's care for faithful is He who promised, "I will never leave thee, nor forsake thee."

June had more than her share of problems by the time she was 18. Her parents were separated but the subject of a divorce never cropped up. The strange thing about it all was that the parents came together for a few days at a time but then went their separate ways again; Mum to her boy friend and Dad to his girl friend. This was particularly tough on June because she was an only child and had no brothers or sisters to whom she could turn.

As she explained to me, she did try very hard to stick to one of her parents as both meant something to her, but they didn't want to know.

Her mother's attitude was, "get off with the old man," whilst her father said, "stay with your mother." June soon got the message that she wasn't wanted and went off to find some lodgings and eventually got herself involved with bad company.

It wasn't long before June was caught shop-lifting and a period of probation followed. From shop-lifting she graduated to house-breaking and burglary and was discovered by the telltale footprints she left beneath a bedroom window. This time the Court heard that she was pregnant and in an act of leniency put her on a further period of probation. It wasn't long before June had an abortion and then she went off with a married man to live in a caravan. That relationship did not last for very long, however, and ended when the man decided to return to his wife.

June was not the sort of girl who would be without a boy friend for long and the next one was insanely jealous of her. He beat her unmercifully and regularly but she stuck to him and often appeared badly bruised and battered. She endured the rough-house treatment for the sake of having a roof over her head because she lived with the young man and his grandmother. In spite of all the ill-treatment she insisted that she loved this fellow and then tried to commit suicide when he eventually went off with another woman.

Then it was June's turn to flit when she got a job she applied for in the North of England. She said I was a friend she could trust and wanted me to go on praying for her. I gave her a Bible the day she gave me her new address and we promised to keep in touch with each other.

Within a fortnight my letter was returned by the Post Office with the envelope endorsed "Gone away" and all efforts to trace her have failed. It's as though she is still on the move looking for love and a permanent home, and there are many kids just like her. Perhaps things would have been so different if just one of the parents had cared.

I often pray that June will read her Bible and discover the love which her Heavenly Father has for her, love like that described in Jeremiah 31 where He says, "I have loved thee with an everlasting love," because there is no love to beat it.

Where love is lacking from a parent to a child it is often amazing to discover that the child has double the amount of love for that parent, it was so in the case of Janice and Bob.

Janice is fifteen and her brother, Bob, a year older. They come from a very good home but the sad part about it all is their mother is an alcoholic.

Father tries hard to keep a good happy home and is the most

patient of all men, but there are many upsets and disruptions in the family life because mother is away from home for days on end.

Janice and Bob are members of my Mission Youth Club and are regularly calling to ask if their mother has been in touch with me. Sometimes she will telephone me from the home of another alcoholic friend to make enquiries of the children, but most of the time no-one knows where she is. She has a host of friends and just moves in with any one of them.

Of the two youngsters, Bob appears to be more concerned about his mother, and he spends hours combing the streets for a glimpse of her. When she returns home from these frequent bouts of absence he particularly does everything he can to please her and to encourage her to stay.

I share his joys when mother has stayed home for a week or two and he assures me that she is never going to leave, then just as regularly I sympathise when he arrives in tears to say she has gone again.

Janice implores me to speak to her mother and I have done so on many occasions. Alcoholics Anonymous have been a great help to her and several of her friends have helped too but several months passed without any sign of improvement: then, suddenly, there was clear evidence of a change for the better in her behaviour. I told Janice and Bob I thought our prayers were being answered and their faith clings to this hope.

Mutual concern for their mother and her problems has drawn Bob and his sister very close together. Here is a case where the circumstances could have had a devastating effect upon these young lives, they have risen up above it and are united in their love and dedication to help their mother win the battle.

I am glad that both Janice and Bob have put their trust in the friend that sticketh closer than a brother. He says, "Fear thou not, for I am with thee: be not dismayed; for I am thy God: I will strengthen thee; yea, I will help thee; yea, I will uphold thee with the right hand of my righteousness." He is able to do just that and make their family joy complete!

Frank knew little of family joy although he too came from a very good home. He was seventeen years of age and had a sixteen year old brother and a fourteen year old sister.

The family is well blessed with material things to the point of luxury and the trio get all they want. May be this is where the problem lies because the youngsters receive everything they ask for, and more beside, and readily admit they do not appreciate their good fortune.

Frank is dissatisfied more than them all and without really knowing why, rebelled against his family. He could not keep a job, became very aggressive and left home to join some hippy friends.

The parents were frantic with worry and tried very hard to get Frank to return, but he refused. The only time he ventured anywhere near the house was when he got into trouble and his father sorted it out, and this was becoming more regular all the time.

It was inevitable that Frank fell foul of the law and ended up in a detention centre.

For the next three years Frank was in and out of centres and finally prison, and it seemed as though all the family just gave up where he was concerned. On one occasion he was in trouble within a week of coming out of prison, then on another occasion he found himself in a police cell on the very day he was released.

I tried to reason with the lad and pointed out the foolishness and futility of his life but he was unrepentant and uncaring.

"You will go back into prison," I chided, "surely you want more out of life than that?"

"Why?" he demanded to know. "It's much better in there than being at home!"

I could hardly believe my ears, something must be very wrong when a young fellow prefers prison to his own home; and sure enough he went back to prison quite happily.

These breakdowns in relationships and everlasting rows and

upsets stem from shaky foundations in family life. To this end my Mission Youth Clubs are more like mission families where we share each problem and try to understand each other. Love must be in the foundation and I can find no better way of expressing it than with Paul in 1 Corinthians 3 – "according to the grace of God which is given unto me, as a wise master-builder, I have laid the foundation, and another buildeth thereon. But let every man take heed how he buildeth thereupon. For other foundation can no man lay than that is laid, which is Jesus Christ." Herein lies the answer!

11

BLESSED ARE THE PERSECUTED

"I KILLED A policeman and lost my driving licence for ten years," the man who was speaking to me didn't look old enough to have held a licence that long in any event.

I was working on a nine day Mission in a couple of small villages and was visiting house to house to encourage folk to come to the nightly Gospel rallies at the Village Hall.

"My friends asked me to drive a car in the East End of London," he went on, "and in all innocence I was happy to oblige. All of a sudden a policeman stepped out in front of us and indicated that I had to stop. I slowed down and one of my mates in the car told me to put my foot down. 'We've got six thousand quids worth of loot on board,' he said, and it was only then I realised I was driving a getaway car carrying jewellery and other things."

He paused for a moment to put the bonnet down on his car and began to wipe his hands on an oily rag. "Well, the copper saw that I wasn't going to stop," he continued, "and jumped on the car, so I decided to brush him."

"Brush him?" I enquired, and the fellow went on to explain. "I just intended to brush him against a wall to knock him off the car, but I underestimated my speed and I killed him."

I noticed how the man kept licking his lips and swallowed quite a bit, it was obvious to me that the memory of it was hurting him still and he fell silent for a while.

"Well I got sent down, of course," he added, "and lost my licence into the bargain. Now I'm away from that life and I want to make a fresh start in the country."

I heard how an influential friend in the district had taken an active interest in him and was prepared to support his application for the return of his driving licence so that he could get a driving job. I wasn't getting anywhere with him on Mission terms I discovered but I wished him well for the future.

As I went from house to house I found the folk very talkative and friendly, talkative that was, on any subject except the local Mission.

Time and time again I heard a similar statement: "The Lord is not interested in the likes of me!" or "I'm not good enough to go to they chapel meetings!" Like the man who had killed the policeman, many of the villagers felt unworthy to go into a place of worship even if it was at the local Village Hall.

The Village Hall in this case was simply called "The Hut" by the local inhabitants. This term described it well since it was a wooden construction about 40′ × 25′ with a small stage at one end and a small coke stove at the other. The entire building stood on short stilts and a very small kitchen appeared on one side as a lean-to.

This little hall was typical of many others in which I have had the privilege of conducting meetings. In the service of rural evangelism it is not at all unusual to take your own water to the premises, light smoky ancient stoves or put up with bucket closets. The buildings are usually draughty and damp, the acoustics are dreadful and the lights are nearly always dim.

In spite of all the draw-backs, however, I have always found the caretakers most helpful in stoking up fires, providing crockery for refreshments and for being on hand at all times to provide everything from electric adaptors to drawing pins. Perhaps I have been more than fortunate in the halls I have hired for Gospel meetings, since I have yet to find one which is not very reasonably priced.

A lot of prayerful planning goes into the preparation of any village Mission. Local churches are invited to share in the special Mission outreach and volunteers are trained to carry out the door to door work.

Programmes have to be worked out in advance so that proper handbills and posters can convey the details, then these in turn have to be delivered to homes or put on display to the best advantage.

Advertisements are placed in the local newspapers and sometimes it is possible to get a mention on a local radio station. But apart from all the advertising by literature there is nothing to compare with the personal approach.

Jesus was a personal worker and this is borne out by His private conversation with the woman at the Well of Samaria, His visit to the man at the Pool of Bethesda and His healing of the daughter of Jairus.

A woman taken in adultery also received a private word from the Lord as did Zacchaeus when he came down from the sycamore tree. There are many other instances on record where Jesus met and spoke with an individual or the ones and twos. We have only to read the Gospels to find in Jesus the perfect example for personal evangelism.

Many folk makes excuses for not coming to Gospel meetings, but, those who do venture always seem to enjoy the informal order of service and voice their appreciation at the close.

A normal Gospel service usually includes two or three hymns, choruses, testimonies of a personal faith in the Lord Jesus Christ, perhaps a solo or group singing accompanied by a piano or a guitar and a Bible reading and a message.

Sometimes appeals are made at the end of a meeting for folk to make a commitment to Jesus Christ, and, there are opportunities to pray for healing of the sick or for any other problem.

God never fails to honour His mission and each one brings a fair share of blessings.

Experience has always shown that a Mission ends when it should be beginning as far as attendance is concerned. It is not uncommon for just a few people to turn up on the first couple of evenings but as the Mission progresses, so the numbers increase. This is particularly noticeable when special answers to prayers have been received and the word spreads around a small community.

I remember one instance when an elderly gentleman was seriously ill in hospital and the son came forward and asked that his father might be prayed for. The following day the son visited his father and found him tucking into his dinner and looking quite well.

At the Mission the following night the son explained how his father had greeted him by saying, "You can see my appetite has come back, I am feeling my old self again and I cannot seem to get enough to eat!"

If we pray believing prayers, should we not expect such an answer? A centurion once said to Jesus, "Say the word, and my servant shall be healed," and when they returned to the house they "found the servant whole that had been sick". The Power of God is still the same and active today and this is what mission is all about.

During one Mission I found a lady, who was an active Christian in the local church, being heavily criticised and persecuted by her husband. Her name was Rose and she told me how he did not share her faith or enthusiasm for Christian things at all. He openly ridiculed her prayers and started to do all kinds of unpleasant things in an attempt to break her down. She went on to say that he wouldn't come within half a mile of the Mission and pleaded with me to pray for husband Bill.

On the fifth night of the Mission Bill had heard just about as much of it as he could stand. After a few pints at the pub he decided to call and collect his wife from the meeting and embarrass her to such an extent that she would not show her face there again. At the same time he would tell the Christians where they could get off. Rose explained all this to me the next time we met.

This particular night, however, as Bill drew near to the Hall he was struck by the sound of a folk singer accompanying himself on a guitar. Bill was a bit of a "folk" man himself and since the singing and playing was first class, he stood outside and listened for some time.

The first time I saw him was when he stepped into the Hall, smoking a cigarette and with the collar of his duffle coat well up around his ears because it was a freezing night.

Looking somewhat confused he edged his way towards the fire at the back of the Hall and stood near it, swaying from foot to foot. Someone went and handed him a hymn sheet but he shook his head without saying a word.

I had no idea that this was Bill but he drew my attention because he was the only member of the congregation to be standing.

I followed the folk singer with a little talk from my hand-written copy of the New Testament, illustrating it by showing the congregation some of the autographs of the famous people who have signed it. The man standing at the back seemed more than a little interested in the signatures and was listening intently to all I was saying.

The moment the meeting ended, the man who had been standing at the back of the Hall strode up to the front and asked me brusquely if he could see the Testament. Turning the front leaves of autographs over rapidly he scanned the pages until he jabbed a finger at the signature of Viscount Montgomery of Alamein.

"I met him," he said, "I was once standing on a runway and he asked me if I was cold because it had been snowing."

As I listened to the incident Rose stepped up beside me. "This is my husband Bill," she said, beaming all over her face, but he only grunted and went on turning the pages of the book. I was delighted to meet him.

Just then the folk singer came along to look at the book as well. Bill asked him how long he had been singing and then got into a technical conversation concerning the guitar.

Rose whispered in my ear, "I can't think what he's doing here. He's been drinking. See if you can have a word with him."

I didn't have a chance to say much, however, because a few minutes later he called Rose and said it was time they went home. I noticed he held the door open for her and she winked in my direction as she left.

A couple of months later I met Rose again at a united Church service. She made her way towards me after the service and greeted me with a grin.

"I thought you would like to know that Bill thought your Mission was very friendly," she said.

"Is that all?" I asked.

"Well at least he didn't disapprove," she replied, "and ever since that night he has never criticised me for going to services again. I cannot persuade him to go with me as yet but it is very much easier for me."

I smiled and reminded her of a couple of verses from Romans, Chapter 8, "If God be for us, who can be against us?" "And we know that all things work together for good to them that love God, to them who are the called according to His purpose."

One seldom sees a large response from a Mission in the rural areas because the folk are few and nearly everyone knows everyone else. For this reason many will not go to a religious meeting for fear of what the neighbours might say, especially if they are not regular worshippers at a church. Proverbs, Chapter 29 describes the situation very well: "The fear of man bringeth a snare: but whoso putteth his trust in the Lord shall be safe."

On this one verse rests or falls most of my purpose for the rural missions, but like the congregations, the labourers are few. I cannot emphasise enough the words of Jesus Himself who said, "Pray ye, therefore, the Lord of the harvest, that He would send forth labourers into his harvest."

We know that on any Mission, one sows, another reaps, but it is always God that gives the increase. The Psalmist encourages us in the work by his words in the One hundred and twenty-sixth Psalm, "They that sow in tears shall reap in joy. He that goeth forth and weepeth, bearing precious seed, shall doubtless come again with rejoicing, bringing his sheaves with him."

12

SEEKING AND SAVING THAT WHICH WAS LOST

"TRAVERS" WAS JUST the house to break into, Ron thought. The old detached house stood behind a large garden on the fringe of the village. There were no neighbours to disturb him and he knew the only occupant was an elderly spinster.

The prospect thrilled him and he felt excitement bubbling up inside as he planned the next move.

He would go round to the back of the house and force a window to get in, just in case someone should suddenly come along and see him in the front garden. Once inside, he would grope about and then take a dekko upstairs. That was it, he would just have a look around and would not in any way disturb the old lady.

Ron didn't intend to hurt anyone and he certainly wasn't breaking in to steal, it was something he had often thought about and now the time was ripe to put those thoughts into action. He would break in, have a look over the house, and depart as furtively as he had arrived. Apart from the forced window no harm would be done, but the fact that someone had been in would spread all over the village next day. Ron liked that, he would be the only one in the village to know who the culprit was and that appealed to a roguish teenager.

Forcing the small back window was an easy task to Ron, he had an uncanny knack of opening the seemingly impossible, it was an art he had learnt earlier on with electricity meters. He slid over the window-sill and slowly edged his way across the dark room.

Seconds later he found the stairs and as noiseless as a cat he ascended step by step, but problems came when he reached the top. First, he banged into a wall and recoiling from that he brushed against a door. The impact caused his breath to escape quite noisily and then a floor-board creaked with every step.

Ron was beginning to sweat as every nerve in his body became taut. There was a small guilt feeling but the very fact that he had got this far without being observed was an achievement. This was just like a television play and Ron was the star. His thoughts were racing as he moved stealthily on feeling his way inch by inch.

His sensitive fingers felt the outline of a door handle and very gently he started to turn it.

"Who's there?" A very frightened voice came from within the room. The unexpectedness of it made Ron freeze with fright and he could literally hear his heart thumping within his chest. He stood quite motionless for some seconds, his hand still outstretched towards the door handle.

"What do you want?" The voice seemed even more afraid and Ron felt desperate. He knew he wasn't going to harm the old lady and he didn't want her to be afraid. Why did she have to be awake just then? Ron cursed inwardly and decided to try and reassure the old lady.

"It's all right, I'm not going to harm you. I'm just going," he said loudly and was just in time to hear her say, "Who are you? What do you want?" as he stumbled to the stairs and ran down them.

He slid over the window-sill much more quickly than when he had got in and then, gulping in great lungfuls of air, he scrambled around the side of the house.

Ron stopped himself from running but walked just as fast as he could to the front gate and slipped through it, then once outside in the deserted village street he began to run for all he was worth.

The lad ran almost all the way to the other side of the village and home. He let himself in, undressed in the dark, and went straight to bed. It was as though he could not get into bed quick enough because it was only then he felt secure.

A thousand thoughts flooded his mind. Did the lady know

who he was? Could she have recognised his voice? He realised he had been very careless where footprints and fingerprints were concerned and he wondered if the police could trace anything to him. He spent a very miserable night and never slept a wink.

Surprisingly enough Ron did not hear anything at all about the break-in the following day or the one after that. He had to pass the house, however, and his eyes swiftly surveyed the front of it as he hurried by. Everything looked quiet and normal, there was no sign of the occupant and he wondered if anything had been done to fix the window at the back.

It was days later when the lady's name was mentioned and he overheard it in the company of friends at a pub.

"Somebody broke in and she heard them," a friend was overheard to say, "whoever it was said they wouldn't hurt her and then they fled."

"Yes, I heard how it made her ill," the second man replied, "I believe she is too frightened to stay there now and she's staying with her sister at Dedford."

"The shock could have killed her," added a third, "if they find out who did it, he should get three years!"

Ron felt quite sick. He knew he didn't want to frighten the old lady and he certainly had not intended to make her ill. He wished there was some way he could explain this to her but he knew this was impossible without giving himself away.

I listened very intently to this story as the lad told it to me. We were sitting by the dying embers at the fireplace in Garfield Hall where one of my three Mission Youth Clubs is held on a Monday evening. All the rest of the members had left long ago but I could see Ron wanted to share his guilty secret with me.

"She did go back to the house after a while," he went on, "but not very long afterwards she died very suddenly."

I was watching his face which was very white and tense. "You know, Ken, I reckon I killed that old lady! She was never the same after I broke in on her and I often wonder if she heard another sound during the night and her heart couldn't stand it."

"Do you think she may have been frightened to death then?" I asked and he was quick with his reply.

"Yes, I reckon she was and when I think about it, I feel like a murderer."

I could tell he meant every word. The death of this lady had had a profound effect on this young man and he was looking to me for some kind of assurance.

"God wouldn't think much of me for such a sin would He?" he asked. "Why don't you ask Him?" I replied, "the Bible is God's word and in it He gives us some marvellous promises."

I instantly led Ron on to see a verse from the first Chapter of the First Epistle to John and followed this from another in Hebrews 10. "If we confess our sins, He is faithful and just to forgive us our sins, and to cleanse us from all unrighteousness," "and their sins and iniquities will I remember no more."

"If you truly repent of the old life and seek God's forgiveness you will get it," I assured Ron, "He will cast your sins into the sea of His forgetfulness and you must forget the incident too."

Paul writing in Philippians 3 says, "This one thing I do, forgetting those things which are behind, and reaching forth unto those things which are before, I press toward the mark for the prize of the high calling of God in Christ Jesus."

"Now why don't you turn that guilty feeling over to God and take His peace?"

Ron did not hand over his problem to God that night but he was in a much happier frame of mind when he left the hall. Months later he did something far better than hand over his problem; on his knees in a little village Chapel he gave God his heart.

I am continually thanking God for giving me the answers to many tricky situations in the three Mission Youth Clubs which I lead as unto Him.

Take for instance the night another young fellow was

bragging to the Youth Club that his girl friend was in trouble. Later, a couple of lads were in earnest conversation with him and I discovered one of the group had a pet theory for solving the problem by inducing an abortion with battery acid. I was horrified to hear such a suggestion but realised these lads were in real earnest.

It took a long time to show these lads the danger and seriousness of the thing they were planning, and the idea was finally scrapped when I vividly described the scene of a murder court. I put as much emphasis into the scene as I could, telling them that such an act would surely kill the mother-to-be and they would be found guilty of her murder. I believe the prospect of a long term in prison and the consequences of the girl's death being forever on their conscience finally won them off the plan. In short, it had to be a clear-cut case of instilling fear into them to avert a tragedy.

Some young folk seem to be quite immune to fear, however, and Reg was one of these types. Reg was a tall and extremely thin lad, aged about twenty, who came to us from a village about ten miles away. He had quite a reputation for fast cars and I shall never forget the night he sat in Garfield Mission Youth Club winding a mass of wires into a small tin-like contraption. On the floor beside him was a large paper bag containing further bits and pieces which little by little he transferred to the tin.

I thought he was making a transister radio and drew near for a closer look. I couldn't make head or tail of it but as I moved away his friend dropped a word which stopped me in my tracks.

Bomb!

No, I must have misheard the word, Reg always seemed to be a peace-loving guy and wouldn't get involved in anything dangerous like that, or would he? What was that strange bomb-like thing he was making? I decided I had better investigate.

"What are you making Reg?" I asked peering over his

shoulder but he didn't reply so I tried again.

"What's it going to be then Reg?"

"I'm making sommat for that old bitch of a Magistrate," he coolly replied, "she fined me fifty quid on a driving offence today but I'll make her pay for it, just you wait and see."

Reg turned his home made bomb upside down and began to plait in loose wire ends with remarkable skill. There was something uncanny in the way he went through the procedure with a hard glint in his eye and his forehead wrinkled in concentration. His features showed rugged determination while his numble fingers continued to play over that lethal tin box.

"Reg, whatever do you intend to do with that thing?" I asked.

"I've found out where the old dear lives who fined me that fifty quid this afternoon," he replied, "and she will not be too keen to fine anyone else when I've lobbed this through her window."

"How much damage can that thing do, Reg?" "Oh its only a little 'un but it will give off a loud bang and frighten the old geezer."

"Say she's by the window when you throw it in, you could kill her with the explosion or even by the shock. What then?"

"Serves her right for being near the window then, don't it?"
"But what if some other innocent person, or say a little child is near the window when its thrown. What is going to happen to them?"

Reg had not considered this possibility before and was silent as he weighed up the situation in his mind. "You know Reg, it's not worth murdering for the sake of fifty pounds," I went on, "apart from having it on your conscience for the rest of your life, you may seriously injure or kill the wrong person."

I watched his face as he took a long hard look at the bomb. He was feeling very sore at being fined so heavily and was hot for revenge. There was no regard for the lady Magistrate at all but I could see he was concerned about the possibility of injuring an innocent victim.

It wasn't long before the contraption, complete with trailing wires and resembling an octopus, was thrown on to the sofa. "I'm fed up," said Reg resignedly, "those old Magistrates have got no idea. My mate was tried at another Court for a lot more offences and he got off a lot lighter. I don't know why some folk get away with murder and others get hammered."

"I'll take charge of this," I said quickly, picking up the tin of wires, "in time you will be glad that you didn't do something stupid which could have got you into a lot of trouble."

"Better get it out of my sight then before I change my mind," said Reg and I was happy to commit the contrivance to the dustbin, thanking God that the possibility of another tragedy had been averted.

All problems are not solved as easily as the one concerning Reg's bomb, however, and some of the difficulties continue year after year.

Many of the young people are violent, addicted to drugs or alcohol, have hang ups on sex or just hate the human race in general.

A "couldn't care less" attitude often prevails, some are unemployed and have no intention of getting a job, whilst others are suffering day after day in jobs they dislike immensely or for which they are totally unsuited. Often boredom or a sense of frustration drives the teenage kids into gangs which tour the district leaving vandalism in their wake, or cause disruptions and fights at local discos and dances, or terrorise the youngsters in other villages.

In the main these youngsters are highly criticised, condemned and harassed, and the old proverb, "give a dog a bad name" is very hard to live down.

Few ever look beyond the character or even try to understand the feelings and fears of the individual. When someone or something is not understood it is so easy to forget it, to become uninvolved, not to bother with the individual's background or care what happens in the future. This is where the Mission Youth Clubs play a very big part and where young people are introduced to Christ who is concerned and cares for every individual. He is the One who will not fail where we so often do.

Luke and Matthew sum the situation up very well indeed as they record Christ's words on the subject in their Gospels. "For the Son of man is come to seek and to save that which was lost" and "They that be whole need not a physician, but they that are sick."

How sad it is when Christians criticise other Christians for associating with the considered outcasts of society, and yet Christ Himself joined on to such in order to bring them unto Himself and to peace and a purpose in life. What clearer picture do we have than His meeting with the prostitute at the Well of Samaria or with the woman taken in adultery!

When Jesus went with Zacchaeus the people said He was gone to be a guest with a man that was a sinner, others referred to Him as gluttonous, and a winebibber, a friend of publicans and sinners. But the fact remains He went and tremendous things always followed His going.

Why then are we reluctant to be involved with the sad cases? Is it because we doubt or limit God's power to help them? Or are we afraid of our reputations being tainted by mixing with undesirables?

"Blessed are they which are persecuted for righteousness' sake:" said Jesus, "for theirs is the Kingdom of Heaven. Blessed are ye, when men shall revile you, and persecute you, and shall say all manner of evil against you falsely for My sake. Rejoice, and be exceeding glad: for great is your reward in Heaven, for so persecuted they the prophets which were before you."

So I rejoice in Mission Youth Club work and I am glad for the many young people whose lives have been wonderfully touched and changed, as frustration and boredom has been replaced by knowing the Person of Jesus Christ. "Wherefore He is able to save them to the uttermost that come unto God by Him, seeing He ever liveth to make intercession for them."

13

BIND UP THE BROKEN-HEARTED

"I CANNOT THINK why Dad is so late coming home for tea," my mother said, "it hardly seems feasible that he went off on his motor-bike at 9 o'clock this morning to get the thing M.O.T. tested and now its nearly 6 o'clock and there's no sign of him."

I could tell Mum was worried. My father had been working on his motor-cycle for days and this day he had taken time off work to take it to an Oxford garage for the test.

"Well he didn't have an appointment," I tried to assure her, "and no doubt he has had to wait a long time before someone could look at the thing."

"The garages would be closed by now," she argued, "and I cannot think why he has not telephoned to say what is happening."

Every few minutes my mother was at the window for a sign of Dad whilst his tea was spoiling in the oven. I was beginning to get anxious too because another hour slipped by without any sign or word from him.

At 7 o'clock a friend called for me to go with him to a committee meeting, and out of earshot of my mother, I told him of my fears for Dad. We decided to go to the village telephone kiosk together where I would 'phone the Oxford hospital to see if he had been admitted by reason of an accident or possible illness. I chose the kiosk because I did not want to add to my mother's fears by telephoning from home.

I got through to the hospital and after being transferred to several extensions I was put in touch with a sister.

"Have you had a Mr. Stallard admitted?" I asked and passed on the relevant information together with our fears for his well-being.

There was a long pause and then I was quizzed on my relationship to Mr. Stallard. I knew by the questions that something was very wrong, especially when she said, "I would go straight home if I were you and someone will be calling to see you!"

I tensed myself and tried again. "You can tell me now whatever it is," I said, "I have someone with me and I should be the one to convey a message to my mother. Has he had an accident?"

Another pause and then the sister said, "I am very sorry to have to tell you Mr. Stallard, your father collapsed and died in the street this afternoon."

I just said "thank you" and vaguely remember replacing the telephone receiver on the rest. A calmness immediately fell upon my soul such as I had never known before and it was as though strong arms were holding me. My friend remembers that my first words were, "I've never felt so much the Presence of Jesus" as we walked from the kiosk to the car and returned home to break the news to my family.

The days that immediately followed the death of my father were confusing and heart-breaking.

A hospital spokesman tried to explain that he died fifteen hours later than he did; another said it was easy to diagnose heart failure in view of the many heart attacks my father had suffered in the past. My father had never had a heart attack or been in hospital in his life!

When we went to see my father the first time it was not convenient for the hospital staff, and, on the second occasion he had been moved to a place of rest awaiting burial. I was handed all his personal effects in a carrier bag but not given the opportunity to see him.

A couple of days later I asked if I was meant to identify Dad, after all he had died in the street and I felt positive identification should be given. I could hardly believe my ears when I was told, "He has already been identified by his son." As I was the only son I knew that was impossible and said so, but all investigations met with red tape and in short, we never saw him dead. All we knew is that that on 12th July 1971, my father, aged 61, left home on his motor bike, apparently in the very best of health, and was never seen again.

All through those confusing and heart-breaking days I felt a real sense of the Presence of the Lord as He shared the burden of my heart, and without exception, I found tremendous comfort every time I opened His Word.

"Peace I leave with you, my peace I give unto you: not as the world giveth, give I unto you. Let not your heart be troubled, neither let it be afraid."

"What I do thou knowest not now; but thou shalt know hereafter."

"Come unto Me, all ye that labour and are heavy laden, and I will give you rest. Take My yoke upon you, and learn of Me; for I am meek and lowly in heart: and ye shall find rest unto your souls."

So I cast my burden upon the Lord and found He was my refuge and strength and a very present help.

With the passing of my father new responsibilities and burdens fell upon my shoulders and complete re-adjustment had to take place in our family life. It was a time of testing but also a time of experiencing Christ with me every moment as He promised, "My grace is sufficient for thee: for My strength is made perfect in weakness."

The days that followed were very full as I took on the new role of bread-winner with added responsibilities for my mother and home, and carried on with my full time secular job and three Mission Youth Clubs, Gospel rallies and weekend preaching. And at this time I really appreciated the warm and loyal support of a seventeen year old friend, Shane, who shared my secular job with the Civil Service. Shared it, that was, for just six short weeks.

The rest of July and most of August slipped by and the August Bank Holiday was a welcome relief from the hectic pressures of the office. Shane, who had worked beside me for two years, insisted that I should take the break and give myself a well earned rest. Neither of us realised it was to be his last.

I took Shane at his word, and with Terry, my co-worker in the Mission Youth work, I went to Hastings to spend the Bank Holiday with our Mission for Christ Rural Evangelist colleagues. It was a time of rich fellowship and spiritual renewal and I felt refreshed to return home and continue in the many things which had fallen to my hands.

Terry and I had left my little van at the car park at Didcot Station and undertaken the trip to Hastings by train, now as we were returning home we spoke of our hopes and aspirations for the future in light of the Scriptural teaching we had recently received.

Alas, our hopes were suddenly dashed when we arrived at Didcot Station and found the little van was no longer at the car park.

I telephoned the police and was told it was at the police station awaiting collection. I was also told that four youths had previously stolen and wrecked it.

We found the van with its roof caved in, the sun shields, mirror and interior light torn off, the big ends knocking because it had been driven for miles without oil, and there was other extensive damage too.

My first thoughts were of dismay, how could we possibly remain mobile for the Lord?

I was able to drive the van but only very slowly because of the knocking in the engine, and by this time I really felt as though I was passing through dark days as one burden seemed to fall upon another.

I returned to the office the following day and was greeted with the news that Shane had had an accident on his motor bike. He had swerved to avoid a pedestrian who had walked out in front of him, and in so doing he fell from the machine. His pillion passenger got up immediately but Shane lay unconscious in the road.

I telephoned the hospital immediately I heard the news and discovered the situation was extremely grave. An hour later I learnt that Shane had died.

So my life took on another period of re-adjustment, changes at home, changes at work, I had lost two of those closest to me and now I was without transport as well. Sympathy flooded in, friends helped, but it was my faith in a God who never changes but loves and cares, that kept me going.

I remember picking up my Bible and reading, "Thou hast beset me behind and before, and laid Thy hand upon me. Such knowledge is too wonderful for me; it is high, I cannot attain unto it. Whither shall I go from Thy Spirit? or whither shall I flee from Thy Presence? If I ascend up into heaven, Thou art there: if I make my bed in hell, behold Thou art there. If I take the wings of the morning and dwell in the uttermost parts of the sea; Even there shall Thy hand lead me, and Thy right hand shall hold me."

That was it, no matter how hard the storms of adversity fell upon me I knew my anchor was founded on the Rock of Ages and He would hold on to me as long as I held on to Him. I also realised that God is no respecter of persons as far as death is concerned; my own father at 61 and Shane at 17 had already been called. No wonder the Scriptures warn us, "Whereas ye know not what shall be on the morrow. For what is your life? It is even a vapour, that appeareth for a little time, and then vanisheth away." But what important decisions we have to make for eternity in that unknown life span, for Christ Himself said, "He that believeth on the Son hath everlasting life: And he that believeth not the Son shall not see life; but the wrath of God abideth on him."

Just prior to this period of trial I had bought a very old caravan for the modest sum of £25·00. It had been offered to me as a bargain and I felt there was a use for it for the Lord.

A farmer friend offered to tow the caravan with his tractor and it eventually ended up in one of his fields in one of the neighbouring villages.

I spent every spare minute renovating and painting the caravan and I was soon very pleased with the result. It had become quite habitable and contained all the facilities of a little home.

One evening one of my Mission Youth Club lads asked me if he could rent the caravan, he had managed to get a good job in the area but was not able to find suitable lodgings. His parents had moved a good distance away and he wanted to use the caravan as a home until he could find something more suitable.

I agreed that he could use the caravan without charge because this lad had been in some trouble and I wanted to encourage him to work and settle down; and the next day he moved in.

From the outset villagers telephoned and warned me that the young man had a girl living with him, but, each time I visited the caravan he appeared to be alone, furthermore he denied all the allegations until a day later I found the girl there myself.

I could not advocate this young unmarried couple living together so I asked the young man to look for alternative accommodation that day. It was a tremendous relief when he said he had found somewhere to live within a few hours.

I could see the caravan was becoming a liability, especially when the farmer urged me to move it from the field. I had asked for a temporary site in the first instance but now I could not find anywhere else where it could be parked. All enquiries to this end failed to produce any answer to my problem and so I advertised it for sale.

No-one, it seemed, wanted an older-type caravan, and the only offer I received was from a Scrap Metal dealer. I agreed to sell him the caravan and it was a happy day when he called at my home to pick me up in his Land-rover to show him where the caravan was parked.

As we drove to the next village the dealer told me his plans for using the caravan and I said I was glad he was going to take it away. But there was a shock in store for both of us, for when we arrived at the field there was no sign of the caravan!

We looked at the dry patch where the caravan once rested and then at each other in blank amazement. I was equally embarrassed and surprised and suggested we went off in search of the farmer for some possible explanation.

The farmer was as mystified as we were at the disappearance of the van, then we discovered from a villager that she had seen someone tow it away with a tractor.

It wasn't long before others confirmed the tractor and towing story, and my scrap dealer friend went off shaking his head without uttering a word. I was left yet again to telephone the police and report some more stolen property.

A day or so later the caravan was found parked on the forecourt of a public house about 20 miles away. The landlord had called to see the caravan when I first offered it for sale but said it was not the type he was looking for. During conversation I dropped a casual remark, "I shall probably be glad to give it away in the end to see the back of it." The landlord interpreted this as a desperate plea on my part and, thinking he was doing me a favour, he carted it away at a later date without so much as a word.

I immediately enrolled the help of Terry, who always seemed to be at my side when trouble struck, and he towed the caravan back again and also managed to sell it on my behalf.

The proceeds from the sale of the caravan helped to put the little van back on the road and once again we were mobile for the Lord. "Many are the afflictions of the righteous" says Psalm 34, "but the Lord delivereth him out of them all."

My afflictions have been many. During one overnight stay at an Earls Court Hotel with a friend, our room was burgled and we lost everything we had. The thief even had the audacity to take away our possessions in our own suitcases.

On another occasion a London taxi-driver drove off with my suitcase of clothes when I hired him to take me to one of the Airport terminals. I left him for just a couple of minutes whilst I went into the terminal to change a five-pound note for my fare, and when I returned to the taxi I found it had gone and so had the case.

Christian friends often remind me of a verse from the book of Job, "Yet man is born unto trouble, as the sparks fly upward," but with the Psalmist I can reply, "But the Lord delivereth me out of them all." There is no problem too difficult for God to handle and no heart-break that He cannot bear. To anyone whe feels heavily burdened as I did when one trial fell upon another, I would say with Deuteronomy 33:27 "The eternal God is thy refuge, and underneath are the everlasting arms."

14

LIBERTY FOR THE CAPTIVES

"WILL YOU PLEASE not talk so fast, I am not writing in shorthand," the Crown Court Judge looked over his spectacles and frowned at me standing in the witness box.

I apologised, and this unexpected interruption made me lose my train of thought, so I began again more slowly.

I was giving a character reference for Darren, one of the Mission Youth Club lads, and his eyes never left me as he sat tense and white faced in the dock.

Darren, along with two others, was accused of a series of thefts and one case of causing grievious bodily harm, and judging by the expressions on the faces of some of the jury members, the case was not going well in his favour.

I had known for some time that this young man was easily led astray by the friends he chose for himself. Most of them had been in trouble and were constantly appearing before the Courts. Darren came from a good home and caused his parents a great deal of anxiety, and it was they who first persuaded him to join the Mission Youth Club.

At first he was reluctant to come, but having once ventured, he enjoyed the warm friendly atmosphere and was always amongst the first to arrive.

"I thought it was going to be all religious," he said, "I didn't realise it was as good as it is, free food and all! I thought you would be preaching all the time."

I explained that each session closed with an epilogue but no-one was obliged to stay although most of them did. I believe Christian actions speak louder than words and the personal help and attention given during the evening probably did more good than a lot of speaking.

Darren agreed, and before very long he had committed his life and energy to Christian service and was very repentant for all the misdeeds prior to his conversion. It was because of the dramatic change in his life, and the help he gave to the Club, that I was prepared to speak on his behalf at Court.

Only the night before he had asked me to pray for him at the Club, and the possibility of a term of imprisonment this time was uppermost in our minds as we prayed. Immediately following the prayer I was led to read to Darren from Acts, Chapter 12 where Peter was imprisoned at the hands of Herod.

Peter's friends had similarly prayed for his release from prison and this came in the form of a miracle. "What God did for Peter he can do for you," I assured Darren and read "Peter continued knocking: and when they had opened the door, and saw him, they were astonished. But he, beckoning unto them with the hand to hold their peace, declared unto them how the Lord had brought him out of the prison."

"Do you think God will prevent me from going to prison then?" Darren asked and I said I felt He would. I was convinced that the lad would be allowed to join us at future prayer meetings.

In this case my prophesy proved to be right and all the lads were given suspended prison sentences and fines. Darren has never forgotten the case which he uses in his testimony of what God has done for him, often emphasising it with a quote from the Book of Hebrews, "How shall we escape, if we neglect so great salvation?"

Andrew, another young Mission Youth Club member, was wonderfully converted from a multitude of problems and worked hard at Bible study and witnessing to his new found faith in Jesus Christ. He was always willing to read, testify, or lead at any service where I was scheduled to preach, and was much sought after by Christian groups. I was concerned, however, that he was on the point of becoming engaged to a girl who did not share his Christian convictions.

"I will lead her to the Lord," he would insist, but I pointed out that this was not an easy thing to do, and, more often than not, it was a case of the uncommitted drawing away the committed.

"I shall never lose my hold on the Lord," Andrew declared, but I had to remind him that Peter the disciple said the same thing to Jesus but then went on to deny Him three times in a single day. I also quoted from I Corinthians 10, "Wherefore let him that thinketh he standeth take heed lest he fall."

Well Andrew was sure of his Christian stand, and I had to confess that I was greatly distressed when his brother told me he had fallen not more than a fortnight later. I received a hasty summons to his home.

Andrew, his mother and I, sat in the front room and bit by bit I pieced together the sorry story. Andrew's girl friend had called him to a crisis meeting concerning the engagement at a village pub the night before. He didn't really want to go to a public house but he assented because the engagement was that important to him.

Whereas the engagement was important to Andrew it was not to the girl friend and she chose that moment to call the whole thing off. There was an argument, voices were raised and the landlord intervened. Andrew swung round on the landlord and hit him, causing the landlord's nose to bleed profusely on to his new pullover.

Naturally the landlord called the police, Andrew was subsequently picked up and driven to the police station where he was charged.

I looked at Andrew and felt sick inside. It was obvious that the affair would be dragged through the Court and the newspapers and all the good work he had done from the pulpit would be undone.

Andrew was by this time heart-broken too at what he had done. He realised how foolish he had been to go to the pub in the first place, he knew he had let the Lord down and lost the girl friend in the bargain. As for me, I knew I had to pick up the broken pieces and hand them back to God. We could still pray and we both knew that the sacrifices of God are a broken spirit and a broken and a contrite heart He will not despise.

After prayer I suggested that Andrew should return to the pub and apologise to the landlord for hitting him, this he did and a sum of money was paid too for replacing the ruined pullover. I drove Andrew to the pub and I knew it took a lot of courage for the lad to speak out as he did.

The landlord was almost in tears and was very sorry that he had called the police when he heard the full story. There was nothing he could do about it, however, since the police were already dealing with the case.

A week or two later Andrew and I were up before the Magistrates, he to plead guilty to hitting a man and I to speak of his conversion and repentance.

The Probation Officer told the Court that Andrew had taken on a Christian hobby and was making every endeavour to be a good citizen. Andrew explained to the Magistrates that he had not taken on a hobby; Christianity meant a new life to him. I was thrilled to hear those words and knew he had returned to a place of God's blessing. This was confirmed when the Magistrates put him on probation and fined him a very small sum.

Outside in the car we thanked the Lord for His Presence in the Courthouse and Andrew said, "I'm not going back there again – ever!" I thank God this is true but I reminded him of very important Scriptures found in 2 Corinthians 6, "Be ye not unequally yoked together with unbelievers: for what fellowship hath righteousness with unrighteousness? and what communion hath light with darkness?"

The newspapers did get hold of the story, of course, and one report was headed "Lapse by Miracle Man" in large capital letters. It gave the whole story including what we had said in Court about prayer, but instead of it having a detrimental affect as far as Andrew's call to the Churches was concerned, just the opposite happened, and that very same day he was on Christian service in Gloucestershire and a month later in

Germany.

It is good to know that, "As far as the east is from the west, so far hath He removed our transgressions from us."

One particular incident which gave me a lot of anxiety at the Mission Youth Club concerned two of its members. Alec and Brian were the very best of friends and when they were not at Club they went to pubs or other places together. Both had similar interests, particularly motor bikes, and they got on well together.

I was very disturbed, therefore, when news reached me that the pair had had a fight in Oxford and Alex had put Brian in hospital with serious injuries.

I looked at Brian propped up in the hospital bed and wondered how one human being could inflict such injuries on another. There was serious damage to Brian's ear and his face was all swollen and black and blue.

I listened carefully as Brian tried to tell me the story with difficulty, and he was still very confused from a terrific blow he had received on his head.

The fight occurred after the couple had been out for a meal with friends, but prior to the meal they had consumed quite a lot of alcohol and this was really the root of the trouble.

Brian said Alec owed him five pounds but Alec denied it. "I gave you a battery for your motor bike," Alec said, "and you accepted it in lieu of the debt."

"The battery was no good and wouldn't fit," Brian replied, "so I'm not accepting it and you still owe me five quid."

The argument went on for some time as Alec considered the debt was paid whilst Brian did not. They were still good friends, however, and on this evening had gone out drinking and for the meal together.

At the end of the meal Alex paid the bill, intending to collect his friends' contribution to it afterwards. Brian saw this as an opportunity to get even with Alec and refused to pay his share towards the meal.

"You owe me that!" he said. "No I do not," was Alec's reply

and another row started between them.

Outside in the street the row got worse until Alec hit Brian in a kind of frenzy and he fell to the ground. Alec was bitterly sorry for his actions the moment his temper cooled and he called a taxi and got Brian home.

Brian's injuries were bad and early the following morning he was whisked off to hospital. The matter was not only very serious by this time, but had become the subject of police action too.

I was in a dilemma to know what to do for the best. I had all sympathy for Brian who was a personal friend as well as one of my Youth Club members, and I had exactly the same relationship with Alec too. I didn't want to side with one or the other, there were obvious faults on both sides but the human suffering involved was quite intolerable. I decided I had to see Alec as soon as possible but not before I had committed Brian to the Master's healing touch and prayer.

Alec sought me before I had a chance to find him. We sat together in Garfield Village Hall one night after all the others had gone. I read the riot act in no uncertain terms and explained Brian's injuries to him at great length.

Alec's eyes were full of tears as he spoke about the forthcoming Court case and expected to go to prison because this was not his first offence.

"I don't mind going to prison, I deserve it," he said, "I just hope and pray that Brian will be all right."

It wasn't difficult to see that Alec's heart was breaking inside although he tried hard to conceal it. He was very worried and concerned that Brian would lose his hearing until we prayed together for the lad.

I knew Alec was more at peace when I spoke to him after the prayer and explained how two debtors in the Bible were dealt with mercifully by the Lord. I quoted, "And when they had nothing to pay, he frankly forgave them both. Tell me therefore, which of them will love him most?"

It was something for Alec to ponder about as he went home.

Some time later I was in the witness box at the Crown Court again to speak about the close relationship these lads had with each other, and to explain how the fight had not been preconceived. It had all happened as a result of drink and a hasty temper.

As I said the words my thoughts went to the first verse of Proverbs, Chapter 20, "Wine is a mocker, strong drink is raging: And whosoever is deceived thereby is not wise."

The case was all over in just a few minutes, in fact it was the shortest time I had ever been in Court. Alec was warned that a recurrence of such behaviour could have serious repercussions and he received a suspended prison sentence.

Brian made an excellent recovery and his hearing was not impaired to the extent we had expected. I was particularly thankful that neither thought any the less of the other because of the incident and as far as I know they are still friends to this day.

"I'm in a spot of bother," Ray looked quite sad as he said it to me whilst I was at the stove cooking the Youth Club supper, "I wondered if you could help me?"

Fishing in his pocket Ray then withdrew a bulky, and all too familiar buff envelope containing his summons to Crown Court.

I read the formidable list of charges which included arson, and this is considered an extremely serious charge by the local Courts and is usually dealt with very severely.

"Tell me what happened Ray," I urged, and out tumbled a strange story.

Ray had been into town to meet his girl friend and during the evening she said she wanted to end their relationship as she had found someone else. The news knocked the young man for six, he could see her mind was made up and all coaxing otherwise was to no avail.

A little later a sad and disillusioned Ray met up with some mates who listened to his tale of woe. They were very sympathetic and invited him to go on a drinking spree with them which he did. Consequently he became the worse for drink and then missed his last bus home.

Ray tried hitch-hiking but was not successful in getting a lift. He carried a bottle of Martini and drank from it as he walked in an effort to ward off the cold.

The more he walked, the more he drank until finally he was exhausted and incapable of going any further. Ray then saw a barn and just managed to stagger inside and collapse on to a heap of straw.

"I must have fallen fast asleep," he said, "the next thing I knew I was very hot and I could hear a lot of crackling. I opened my eyes and I could see flames everywhere. I got out of the barn and was staggering about the field when some people came running towards me; then later the police picked me up."

There had been several arson cases in the area about this time and Ray found himself very high on the suspect list for all of them. This implication bothered Ray a lot and he insisted that he was innocent of setting fire to anything deliberately.

"I did not go into the barn intending to set it alight," Ray went on, "I don't even know if I lit a cigarette as I was so far gone." So was it arson or could it have been an accident? We had to wait for the Court to decide.

I was called as a character witness and, as usual, we prayed about it the night before.

Ray realised that the Judge on his case was well known for handing out severe punishment, and as he had committed other offences, he considered he was in for a hard time. It appeared that the Judge was reported in the newspapers that week as sentencing the wrong-doers to terms of imprisonment and Ray thought he might well follow suit.

After prayer, the lad said he felt more calm, and then made an amazing statement.

"The Lord will be with me," he said, "and the sun will shine too."

The weather was going through a very dull time and the sun

had not been seen for some time. It hardly seemed possible that it would re-appear just then.

I arranged to meet Ray and his parents at the Town Hall where the Crown Court was to be held, and Ray was really dreading his appearance before the severe Judge. But when I got to the Town Hall none of them were there!

I soon discovered that due to the volume of cases to be heard that day, Ray's had been transferred to the Crown Court at the County Hall, and he was to appear before a Judge well known for leniency. Many of the Youth Club members would call this a good stroke of luck but I would call it answer to prayer.

When I arrived at County Hall there was a mix up concerning my call to the witness box to speak about the lad and his behaviour at the Club. I was forgotten, and as I patiently waited outside to be called, Ray and his parents emerged from the Court. The case had been heard and it was all over. He simply had to pay a fine!

I shook hands with them all and we made for the exit. As we stepped through the door we walked into brilliant sunshine, and turning, Ray grinned from ear to ear and said, "I told you so!"

Ray and his mother were so thankful that prayers had been answered that they both asked if they could travel with me to my preaching engagement the following Sunday. It was 30 miles away but it was a great pleasure to be able to take them.

I often think how Ray was terrified at the prospect of appearing before the Judge. It is a sobering thought that one day many will appear before God as their Judge for in Revelation 20 it is written, "And I saw the dead, small and great, stand before God; and the books were opened: and another book was opened, which is the book of life: and the dead were judged out of those things which were written in the books, according to their works."

I am so thankful that I am the witness and not the accused at these Court proceedings. I am glad too that my charge of sin has been dealt with by Jesus who bore it in His own body on the Cross. I deserve hell punishment for sin but Jesus paid the penalty in His Blood and I go a free man.

"If the Son therefore shall make you free, ye shall be free indeed," Jesus said, and I agree without reserve.

15

FIELDS WHITE UNTO HARVEST

THERE WERE TWO loud bangs, a horrible scraping sound and a bump, sufficient indications to tell us that the silencer had fallen off the van.

Terry and I were on our way to a small village Chapel where I was due in a few minutes to take the evening service. To add to the silencer problems was the fact that we were driving through a thunderstorm.

"Stop the van and I'll fix the silencer," Terry said, "it will be better than you having a go and getting yourself all messed up before you speak to the people."

We pulled up at a lay-by and Terry stepped out into the pouring rain. He got down on his hands and knees and tried hard to replace the offending piece of pipe which by this time was very hot.

With one eye on my watch and the other on the rain I sat and patiently waited. "Oh leave it, Terry," I said, "we will just have to go on without it, there's no time to fix it even if the rain stopped."

The van spluttered into life again and off we went with a great deal of noise.

We almost frightened the lives out of a couple of cyclists we passed, the van was making a dreadful row and each time the accelerator pedal was pressed the volume of noise increased.

The Chapel steward was looking out for us since we only had a couple of minutes to spare before the service was due to commence.

"You can park there!" he said and pointed to a nice lawn at the side of the Chapel where we duly brought the van to rest.

As we walked to the building I felt very conscious and a little ashamed of our noisy vehicle.

"As soon as the service is finished we will make a hasty departure," I whispered to Terry, "I don't want the whole congregation to witness our noisy old van so we will leave before they come out of the Chapel."

Sure enough, as soon as I had finished preaching and shook hands with the congregation, I indicated to Terry that we would make a hasty exit. Once outside the Chapel, we ran to the van and Terry quickly switched on the ignition. That was when our problem really started!

The van literally roared into life but we couldn't budge an inch. With all the rain we had had the van had sank up to its axles in thick mud and we were stuck fast.

The more Terry tried to accelerate to get us out of the mud, the more we sank into it but more worrying was the increased noise through the lack of the silencer. And the rain continued to pour, and I was getting concerned because the congregation started to leave the Chapel headed by the steward.

"Our brethren are stuck in the mud," he said, "come on, let's give them a push."

To my dismay a retinue of folk in Sunday best bore down on our little van, and the steward gave instructions as to who should stand where to give the most effective push.

The pushers heaved, the van accelerated with a noise which almost pierced the ear-drums, the wheels spun at an alarming rate and the van back-fired with a sudden shower of mud. Simultaneously we shot forward, and out of the back window I caught a glimpse of the mud spattered congregation.

I don't think either of us will ever forget the look of surprise or the expression on the face of the lady organist. Her beautiful pink coat and matching hat were caked with thick mud, she had got a mouth full too and was spitting for all she was worth.

A bewildered bunch of folk, looking decidedly dejected, waved but not very enthusiastically as we roared away. Sometimes I wonder if this little episode has anything to do with the fact that we have never been invited back again!

I enjoy my evangelistic ministry to the rural areas, it is tough work but there are many blessings attached to it. I am very conscious that the church in the rural areas of Britain is witnessing a continual decline although twelve and a half million souls live in such areas.

It is all too common to find country communities without any form of Gospel witness, Sunday School or Youth Club. Only a few elderly believers are found in many places of worship which often lacks any regular fellowship, Bible study or prayer meetings. Consequently the knowledge of the Scriptures is limited and folk are unable to relate Bible teaching to their daily living.

Having lived all my life in villages I am burdened for the souls of village folk. At the present rate of decline there will be no places of worship left for them to attend in a few years time, more than 700 village churches were closed in one year alone. So there is something very urgent about the message of Romans, Chapter 10. "How then shall they call on Him in whom they have not believed? and how shall they believe in Him of whom they have not heard? and how shall they hear without a preacher? and how shall they preach, except they be sent? as it is written, How beautiful are the feet of them that preach the Gospel of peace, and bring glad tidings of good things!"

Taking the Gospel to villagers is a vital task but can also be one of humour or heartbreak. It gives occasion for many interesting conversations and unusual incidents but one often requires the wisdom of Solomon and the patience of Job.

I have spent many hours trailing around gardens to look at giant marrows, prize sweet peas or laden fruit trees in the course of calling at homes with the Gospel. I have lost count of the times I have been introduced to dogs, cats, calves and chickens and sometimes I have even been called upon to perform the services of a vet!

I called on one elderly lady who was struggling with a duck

and a roll of adhesive tape. "Will you hold the duck?" she asked, "its leg is broken and I want to put it in a splint." I duly obliged and ended up holding the duck and fixing the tape.

As I approached another front door I could hear a female voice calling somewhere from the back. "Can someone help me please? Please help me!"

I hurried to the back of the house and found a lady standing on a chair. While she was attempting to clean her windows, the sash cord had broken, letting the top window down suddenly and trapping her fingers between it and the bottom. This time it was a case of first aid and the making of a cup of tea.

Regular visits build up a friendship and often lead to the sharing of personal problems and hospitality. It is not unusual to consume half a dozen cups of tea in as many homes during one afternoon of visiting, and to consume food ranging from a biscuit to a lump of bread pudding. It is little wonder therefore, that rural evangelists often have to watch their weight!

Whilst some may be watching their weight, I am always on the lookout for any interest in spiritual things. On one occasion I was rather surprised to be asked to pray for a cow that was ill, a grandmother who was poorly and a mother who had a nasty boil. The following week I asked if my prayers had been answered. "Oh yes," I was told, "grandmother is fit and well now and mother's boil has completely gone!"

"What about the cow?" I enquired, "is it all right?"

"Oh yes, she's all right," was the chirpy reply, "she's dead!"

What could I do but praise the Lord for two answered prayers and then quote from Job, "The Lord gave, and the Lord hath taken away; blessed be the name of the Lord?"

One particular Sunday I was blessing the Name of the Lord as I was getting a Chapel ready for an afternoon service. I had raked all the ashes out of the ancient coke stove and lit the wood and coal which I laid at the bottom of the thing.

It was usual to wait for about half an hour for the coal to burn sufficiently before the coke could be added, so I whiled away the time by playing the pedal organ.

At the sound of music a small boy appeared and sat and listened as I played, and he remained quite silent until the chimes of the ice cream van could be heard outside; then off he went as quickly as his little legs could carry him.

I sat with my back towards the door and continued to play as the Chapel slowly filled with smoke emitted from the many holes in the stove.

Soon the Chapel was full of smoke and it was as though I was now pounding the organ for all I was worth to rise above this irritation. I was giving the instrument full swell, more jazz than sacred, when the door behind me opened and I guessed the little lad with the ice cream had returned.

"You seem to be having fun!" I heard an unfamiliar voice behind me and I swung round to discover three clerics including a bishop all staring at me.

I jumped down from the organ and made my way towards them.

"As it's Rogation Day we are touring the village and blessing the crops," the vicar explained, "and as the Bishop is visiting us today, and we were passing and saw your car outside, I thought I would introduce you!"

I started to utter my apologies for not being able to shake hands, I was embarrassed that they were still dirty from the fire lighting, conscious all the time too that we were all breathing in more than our fair share of fumes and thick black smoke.

As I stood feeling most awkward and wondered how I should explain away the smoke, the door opened for the second time and the small boy re-appeared with two ice cream cornets. He completely ignored my three distinguished visitors and promptly thrust one of the cornets into my hand with a quick, "you owe me 5p!"

The bishop smiled. "It's so nice to meet you," he said, "but I see you are very busy and we must not detain you. Goodbye and God bless you!" and off they went as noiseless as they had come.

I felt miserable after the trio had left, it had been a very kind gesture on their part to visit the nonconformist Chapel but I felt I had been most inhospitable. It was some time later that I thought of three wise men who visited not a smoky but probably smelly cattle shed at Bethlehem almost 2000 years ago. They had travelled a great distance to present their gifts to the infant Jesus. Well now, smoke or no smoke, I was still endeavouring through it all to present Jesus to the people because He said, "I am not come to call the righteous, but sinners to repentance."

Village evangelism would hardly seem to be a dangerous mission field but I have encountered many hair raising incidents.

As I travelled to one village I met a young man who was called Tim working on a farm. His parents were divorced and he lived alone in a very old caravan which was situated in a very isolated spot across some fields.

I took the lad to meet some friends of mine and during the evening they told him that it was impossible for them to go away on holiday because they had an alsatian to look after.

"I can look after the dog," my young friend said, "it will be company for me at the caravan."

My friends took him at his word and Rex was duly driven to his new home the following Thursday.

On the Sunday that followed I called to see Tim at the caravan but he was not at home. What I did find, however, was a very ferocious Rex.

The dog snarled and snapped its teeth as it threw itself at the door of the caravan and I could see through the window that it was pacing up and down looking like a lion in captivity. There was no way I could open the locked door and I assumed the intense heat of the summer day was bothering the animal.

I searched for Tim but I could not find him, and had to give up after a short while because I was on my way to take a service and I was restricted for time.

The following morning Tim telephoned.

"I want you to do me a favour," he began, "I am at Carlisle and I want you to look after a dog at my caravan."

"What are you doing there?" I asked, and he explained how a girl friend had intended to hitch-hike to Cumberland the previous Friday.

"I didn't think it was safe for her to hitch-hike all those miles," said Tim, "so I brought her here in my car and I have decided to stay here for a few days too."

It suddenly dawned on me why I had found the alsatian so ferocious the previous day. It had been imprisoned in a sweltering caravan for three days and now it was going into four.

I proceeded to tick Tim off for his cruel and inconsiderate actions when the pips sounded and he rang off. The call had come to me at the office and a lady colleague was all for reporting the matter to the R.S.P.C.A. as I made for home to get water to take to the dog. Tim had said I would find plenty of tins of dog food under the caravan.

With a thumping heart I approached the caravan and found the key hidden in its secret place with the food, and, at the sound of my footsteps the dog started barking and tearing at the door with its claws.

We have never had a dog at home, neither was I confident when I came anywhere near them. In this instance I was very scared, and reluctant to open the door and get near the animal.

I decided to open the door very slightly and Rex, sensing freedom, stuck his head through the crack and then started thrusting his body forward for all he was worth. I suddenly opened the door wide and as he sprang out I jumped inside and slammed it shut. It was now a case of the dog being on the outside and me on the inside!

The caravan reeked of excrement and urine and there was not a drop of water to be found except for that which I had taken with me. I tried to open one of the tins of dog meat with a rusty can opener but it broke before I was able to complete the job. In an attempt to pull the tin open I ripped my fingers and the blood began to drop all over the place; even so it did not stop me pulling out the meat and tossing it out of one of the windows for the dog.

Rex sprang at the meat and wolfed it down in great mouthfuls and I found him some biscuits as well. He would insist on running into the corn and sniffing and for a time seemed quite dazed by his new found freedom.

By and by I was not feeling quite so afraid of the dog and I gingerly filled the bowl with water and placed it on the caravan step. It was gone in an instant so I refilled it again twice before he seemed satisfied.

Then I found myself having agonising thoughts and wondered whether I should have given the animal the drink first. An evangelist may well be all things to all men I decided, but I was certainly out of my depth as far as animals were concerned.

In order to give the dog maximum exercise I stayed at the van for three hours and cleaned it from end to end to keep myself occupied.

Later it was no easy task to persuade Rex to get back into the van but at last the task was complete and I made sure it was left with adequate fresh air, food and water until I could return the following day.

A couple of days later I received another telephone call from Cumberland, this time it was a Minister to tell me that Tim was in hospital as the result of taking an overdose of tablets.

'He is very depressed,'' the Minister said, ''and I understand his caravan life is not all it should be. Can you do anything for him?''

I promised to paint the interior of the caravan and undertook to get all Tim's clothes washed and ironed, assuring the man that I would do everything possible to welcome the lad and to keep an eye on him when he came home. So every night for the rest of the week I spent hours working on the caravan whilst Rex romped all round it, seemingly no worse for his ordeal just a few days previously. I enjoyed every minute of the countryside and eagerly looked forward to seeing Tim's face when he saw the transformation of the van. Well I was soon to be disappointed on that score as Tim suddenly appeared on my doorstep one morning.

"Have you got my clothes?" he asked and I fetched him his things all nicely washed and pressed. I could tell he was very pleased to find them so.

"Have you seen your caravan yet?" I asked and was staggered by his reply. "Yes, thanks for what you have done on it, Ken, but you need not have bothered, I am not going back there anymore!"

I was so surprised that I didn't utter a word. Tim smiled and went on. "I've got a couple of friends waiting for me outside who would like to meet you. They are a young married couple and they have invited me to live with them."

Five minutes later Tim and his new found friends had gone and I've never seen them since, neither could I discover what happened to the caravan which suddenly disappeared.

Some folk would say it was a wasted week, a lot of effort for nothing, but that is not strictly true. It did teach me a lesson on grace and gave me a clearer understanding of what Paul the apostle meant when he wrote in Romans 5, "Therefore being justified by faith, we have peace with God through our Lord Jesus Christ: By whom also we have access by faith into this grace wherein we stand, and rejoice in hope of the glory of God. And not only so, but we glory in tribulations also: knowing that tribulation worketh patience; and patience, experience; and experience, hope." Anyway it was not a waste of time because Rex and I got closely acquainted, and we both went to our homes trusting each other so that I have never been afraid again of one or visiting a home where there is a dog.

Visiting homes with the Gospel is not easy but at least it gives people a chance to accept the Saviour. Jesus said "Go ye into all the world, and preach the Gospel to every creature," and that includes isolated farms and folk in the smallest hamlets.

Then when souls are won to Christ the work is not finished, each must be encouraged to worship and to go on in the Christian life. There is Bible teaching to be done and prayer meetings to foster, the sick to be visited and problems to discuss. A rural envangelist often has to be a counsellor and a friend, ready to take on any given task in the Strength of his Lord.

Not all Christians are happy to weed, cut grass or paint at the house of the Lord, some are not willing to undertake the menial tasks like washing up or lighting a fire, but all of these things are necessary and important to God. I find much blessing comes to me in the less spectacular jobs as I try to be faithful in the smaller things.

The Scriptures encourage me:

"For God is not unrighteous to forget your work and labour of love, which ye have shewed toward His name, in that ye have ministered to the saints, and do minister."

"And let us not be weary in well doing: for in due season we shall reap, if we faint not."

"Therefore, my beloved brethren, be ye steadfast, unmoveable, always abounding in the work of the Lord, for as much as ye know that your labour is not in vain in the Lord."

16

CHRISTIAN INFLUENCE

LITTLE ANGELA LOOKED up into my face and with complete sincerity said, "I was given fifty pence for my birthday and I want to give it to Jesus."

The happy face which accompanied the offer of money tugged at my heart and I accepted the gift for the missionary box with many kind words of gratitude.

It was not my intention to deprive the six year old of her birthday present but I knew there were ways of repaying the fifty pence, so that her gift would not appear to have been rejected. God, who is no man's debtor loves a cheerful giver, and we know that if we cast our bread upon the waters, it will return to us after many days.

Three youngsters, two eight year olds and one a year older, burst into the Good News Club to announce they had been carol singing. The older boy thrust a rusty toffee tin into my hand and I was amazed to find it almost full of coins.

"Can you send this to a Childrens' Home?" he asked "we have been carol singing for poor children. Shall we help you count the money?"

With very cold fingers the little trio helped me to count four pounds and forty pence. "We will make that up to Five pounds," I said and their faces glowed with delight. Even so, their moment of pleasure was small in comparison to mine, which continues all through the year in teaching two small groups of children in separate villages.

I taught a Sunday School for Garfield children every Sunday morning in the Village Hall because there was no non-conformist church there. The small Anglican church, a sister church to a larger one in another village, was opened for half an hour once a month only for a service of Holy Communion. Apart from this, there was no spiritual food to be had in the village and I felt led of God to supply in the famine.

Some time later I was led to re-open a church in a very large village about six miles away. The latter field of service called very heavily upon my time with Sunday School, Youth work, Prayer Meetings and the Sunday services. At that time I was also organist, secretary and treasurer.

The Lord richly blessed this new ministry and the numbers increased, as did the weekly tasks, until I found that I could no longer cope time-wise with the two Sunday Schools.

I was not led to close down the first children's ministry at Garfield but after much prayer, I was given the answer.

Sunday School would continue at my recently opened new church and instead of Sunday School at Garfield, a "Good News Club" would be held for an hour at the Village Hall on Monday evenings. This would be followed immediately by the teenagers' Mission Youth Club, which would all take place in the same Hall around the cheery fireside. So for several years now, the Garfield children come for an hour and as they leave, the youth arrive. Although this is a very exacting and tight arrangement, it has proved to be a real blessing and keeps the childrens' meeting going in that village.

I view childrens' work as special and very important. Christ rebuked His disciples when they refused children and He used them to illustrate spiritual truths.

"And Jesus called a little child unto Him, and set him in the midst of them, and said, Verily I say unto you, except ye be converted, and become as little children, ye shall not enter into the Kingdom of heaven.

"Whosoever therefore shall humble himself as this little child, the same is greatest in the Kingdom of heaven. And whoso shall receive one such little child in My name receiveth Me." St. Matthew 18.

Many Sunday School teachers become frustrated in their attempts to keep law and order in the class. Discipline is a must but this is often lacking in the home and consequently is difficult to introduce or maintain in Sunday School.

Parents often fail to realise the importance of discipline, although the Bible has much to say about it. One of the most familiar is, "He that spareth his rod hateth his son; but he that loveth him chasteneth him betimes." (Proverbs 13:24.) Now this passage is sometimes misinterpreted but it lays the foundation for guiding a child in the right direction because discipline includes punishment.

It is vital for any teacher to observe that with punishment must be given the knowledge of forgiveness and love. A child needs to understand that he is still very much wanted and should be treated as an individual.

Well, having introduced a pattern of discipline, what then are we to teach the child? In this respect I have found considerable difficulty in finding teachers in the villages, so that it has been necessary to amalgamate in one class an age group from six to fourteen.

Prayer is my only answer to this problem, for without it my lessons would be too "babyish" for the older pupils or over the heads of the younger ones.

All children love a story and this is a good place to begin, but, care must be taken to see that it is Bible based. I have found it helpful to hold a quiz on the passage read or the content of a story, awarding points for correct answers. It is amazing how the smaller details are remembered in this way and it encourages the child to concentrate on the subject in hand.

Too often children are considered to be "just children" when all the time they are observing relationships, grasping serious matters and being influenced for good or bad.

It is essential that any adult leader should maintain high standards, never talk down to a child and be extremely fair in all his dealings. Children respect adult authority and often look up to the leader as a hero.

I know of an instance when a minister told a youth he was

looking bored. "I should stay away if you are bored with it," he said, and the youngster never entered the church again. Whenever the lad's family or Christian friends encouraged him to go to a service, he would say, "The minister said I need not go." I am sure the minister never realised that his careless statement could have such an effect on that young person's attitude to the church or indeed upon his life.

"Lo, children are an heritage of the Lord: and the fruit of the womb is his reward." Psalm 127:3.

Experience has taught me to avoid at all costs a set routine in the religious education programme. My classes are taught the Scriptures and how to pray and praise. Reverence for God and practical Christianity also rate high in the list of priorities.

To avoid a set routine I keep up the interest in Christian things by participation projects. Village children enjoy simple changes and during the summer months we often go swimming and then sit by the riverside for the lesson. Sometimes we go out into a field and play ball games before sitting down on the grass to read together; thus surrounded by nature one has ample scope to illustrate spiritual truths.

Full use is made of the time and seasons. Every Maundy Thursday afternoon we go for an Easter Egg Hunt when the children search a field and the hedgerows for their chocolate treats. This little occupation led me to realise that this afternoon of fun need not be restricted to Maundy Thursdays only, so consequently we go off on treasure hunts and hide and seek from time to time. In this way the schools have something to look forward to in their programmes and they appreciate it so much that they work three times harder in the serious Christian things which really matter.

Parents and other adults are quite easy to reach through the children too. If a class is encouraged to participate in the Sunday School or Good News Club Anniversary, you can almost guarantee that the parents and friends will be there to watch or encourage. Similarly summer trips or Christmas parties are opportunities to welcome the older members of families. Several of my congregation first came into church contact through similar means, they enjoyed the friendship and then started coming to services on a regular basis.

Christian film shows, sales of work for class funds, and barbecues are all ways in which folk can be contacted.

The Bible says, "Go out into the highways and hedges, and compel them to come in, that My house may be filled," and again, "I am made all things to all men, that I might by all means save some."

Not all the influences which come into Christian service can be beneficial I am sorry to say.

I remember one particular coach trip to the seaside. A large tourer was duly ordered and the Mission scholars eagerly booked their seats along with parents and friends. Two or three days prior to the trip I still had a few vacant coach seats to fill, and a traveller who had already booked asked if her friends, a young married couple and two small children could come too. I readily agreed although I did not know the family.

The day started well and the coach was full, but we had not gone very far before the mother of this little family appeared to get very noisy. I was disturbed to hear bawdy singing and swear words and decided I should speak to her. I discovered that she had consumed almost a bottle of gin before we had got half way to the sea.

The lady's behaviour was obviously causing annoyance to the passengers sitting near to her and was an embarrassment to say the least in front of the children. I was glad when we arrived at the sea and went our different ways.

Sadly there was worse to come. During the afternoon we met some friends on the promenade and they had just seen the lady from our coach being bundled into a police car and whisked away. I felt shattered by this piece of news and began to wonder what would happen at the coach departure time.

Everyone arrived promptly except the family, of course, and suddenly the husband appeared and called me on one side.

"Can you get the driver to call at the police station and pick up my missus?" he asked, and so off we went on a tour of the city to find it. Round and round we went as each time we stopped to ask the way, someone gave us a different direction.

Eventually we found the police station and collected our passenger who was still very much the worse for drink. This did not stop her taking more alcohol on the way home, however, or finally leaving the coach at a public house when we returned to the village.

I realised that day how active an agent the devil is as he tried to wreck the service of the Lord. You don't have to teach a child to do wrong, that comes easily enough, but it is hard and painstaking work to teach him the right. Today's children are tomorrow's adults, so how much the Lord needs dedicated Christian workers for Sunday Schools today! To those already working in such an important sphere of service, may you be encouraged by the words of Jesus who said, "Suffer little children to come unto me," and again, "My mother and my brethren are these which hear the word of God, and do it."

17

WALKING THROUGH THE VALLEY

THE LITTLE OLD lady peered up at me and then did two things simultaneously, she spat directly into my face and hit me on the head with her rolled newspaper.

I was making my usual monthly visit to a geriatric hospital a few miles away from home. A beautiful country mansion ideally situated and surrounded by lovely gardens and lawns has been converted into a hospital for the elderly.

Most of the patients spent the majority of their time in their little low cot-like beds, whilst others got up for a few hours each day and just sat and looked out of the windows or rested quietly in the garden on fine days.

A third group was fairly fit and well but were incapable of looking after themselves, for this reason they lived together as a community, helped with the daily chores around the hospital, and in the evenings sat together watching television in a spacious and nicely furnished sitting room. We called this little group "The Ramblers" since they were able to ramble at will about the hospital and grounds and even further afield.

At the hospital my ministry was mainly to this little group. A party of us went along occasionally but most months I went alone to sing hymns with the patients, read to them from the Bible and to preach a short gospel message.

The visits were always warmly received as those dear folk loved to choose their favourite hymns. We met in an atmosphere of warm friendship and each meeting was very informal.

The climax of the meeting came when the little mixed congregation of men and women, although the women far outnumbered the men, reached out for their favourite sweets and

Christian magazines which we took along. Sometimes a patient asked for a Bible or requested prayer, and each successive year made the work more vital and worthwhile.

I wiped the spittle from my face and tried again with this little lady.

"How are you today?" I asked, but all I got was a murderous look and then, clutching her handbag tightly by the handles, she said, "You are not going to steal any of my money."

It was only when I explained we did not take any money that she began to relax but I noticed she kept a tight hold on the handbag.

"What sweets have you brought?" she asked and I said these would be distributed at the close of our little meeting; she snorted, leaned back in her chair and closed her eyes. I knew I had been dismissed and moved on to the next lady.

Some of these friends were very confused and I was often taken for a son or a grandson. All the explaining in the world was to no avail so I simply sat and listened to family talk and humoured the old folk.

It was not unusual for at least one of the patients to cut right into the middle of the sermon to say such things as "I've been on holiday," or "Have you got any flowers in your garden?" It was all very sweet and the joy which was shared in those little meetings was very rewarding.

Petty squabbles often flared up because they sat for so long together and got on each others nerves. Disputes arose over who wanted what on television channels, and then some wanted to sleep when others were being over-active.

It was good to see the handicraft work and much of the needlecraft and basketry is very well done, this helps to pass away the time which otherwise would hang very heavily on their hands.

Some of the cases were very sad and I never left the hospital without a burden on my heart for at least some of them. The patients talked of sons and daughters who had not been near them for years. I was shown letters and photographs which had been sent along but these do not take the place of a personal visit.

One photograph showed a woman of forty-five ablaze with happiness on the arm of the husband she had just married. The mother was in tears because she had not received an invitation to the wedding and had not seen the daughter since she was thirty. The daughter had written occasionally during the years but had not once visited the mother in all that time. I found this was quite common and it was very unusual to see a visitor during visiting hours on a Sunday afternoon.

It was just as though those dear souls were forsaken and almost forgotten by their families, and in the case of the recently married daughter, she lived less than forty miles away from the hospital.

In these circumstances I usually speak of the loving Father's care and concern and commend them unto His love and keeping, bearing in mind the admonition of James, Chapter 1, "Pure religion and undefiled before God and the Father is this, to visit the fatherless and the widows in their affliction, and to keep himself unspotted from the world."

Even so, I am convinced that many families do not realise the heart-break they bring to their parents and relatives in hospital and a once in a while effort to visit would mean so much to them.

There are instances when Christians fail to visit their relatives too and this is inexcusable in light of the words of Jesus Himself who said, "I was an hungred, and ye gave me no meat: I was thirsty, and ye gave me no drink: I was a stranger and ye took me not in: naked, and ye clothed me not: sick, and in prison, and ye visited me not. Then shall they also answer Him, saying, Lord, when saw we Thee an hungred, or athirst, or a stranger, or naked, or sick, or in prison, and did not minister unto Thee? Then shall He answer them, saying, verily, I say unto you, inasmuch as ye did it not to one of the least of these, ye did it not to me."

Where families and relatives failed, the Matron and staff more than compensated and worked together as an efficient team. Their love and patience was exemplary and not only did it flow to all the patients, but to us too on every visit.

In those early days of visiting this hospital we used to meet on a ground floor and sing with piano accompaniment. When the sitting room was tranferred upstairs we lost the piano and this was a matter of concern for Clara.

Clara loved the piano and often spoke of her own which at that time was in the care of her nephew.

One evening she wrote on a postcard to ask the nephew to send the piano to the hospital. I was instructed to stamp the card and post it, which I did.

This procedure went on for over a year and although I tried to dissuade the lady from sending any more cards, I was forced to by her insistence. Not one single card was ever acknowledged and consequently we never saw any sign of the piano.

Emma once worked for a titled family and her poor mind was so confused that she still considered she was with her employers. She conversed with a Duchess all the time until eventually you could almost see one sitting next to her. The actual conversations were so intelligent that it was hard to understand she was really talking to herself.

Harry was extremely nervous and shy and spent most of the time staring at the carpet, but his friend Tom was just the opposite, commandeered most of the hymn requests before anyone had time to think and was not averse to a few choice swear words every now and then.

Everywhere we looked we could see a need and this led us to lengthy times of prayer. We knew our monthly visits were enjoyed and very much appreciated, but this was only a drop in the ocean. These dear ones needed more visits and entertainment and the hospital staff were wonderful in their tireless efforts to encourage these things.

As the months slipped by it was noticeable that our Rambler

congregations were getting smaller. The older and more infirm members were transferred to the geriatric wards where they received more attention, and the fitter patients went off to a community home in town. We missed them, of course, but it was good for them to be able to live in a home environment rather than a hospital situation.

My heart is burdened in that more churches and individual Christians could do more for the elderly. This particular hospital is fortunate to have several visitors and practical help from the St. John's Ambulance Brigade. Members of the Brigade willingly undertake general nursing duties, they help to feed patients and to lift them in and out of bed, apart from many other interesting tasks. But why should these things be left to a few?

Hospitals can always do with more willing helpers, especially at weekends when there is usually a shortage of staff. This is an ideal time to visit and a golden opportunity to take someone for a short car ride or even for a walk in the grounds.

To know that someone cares is very important to elderly folk and their time is made all the more pleasant if they know in advance that someone is going to visit them. How they love to have something to look forward to!

Experience has taught me that the majority of senior citizens are not very interested in television or reading. Books very often lay unopened but they love to chatter. I found also that the elderly folk just adore children and are quite happy to converse with them for hours. Anyone visiting a geriatric hospital with children, but not small babies, can be assured of a very warm and rewarding welcome.

Since hospital visitation brings so much joy to the patients, this is one avenue of ministry I would not like to drop. I believe so many more could be engaged in this type of ministry if only they would pause long enough to consider the vast amount of time Jesus spent in the company of sick folk. The plea of the impotent man of St. John, 5 still cries out today, "Sir, I have no man, when the water is troubled, to put me into the pool."

Visiting the bedridden is a sad task and is not one I can undertake easily without a lot of prayer beforehand.

So many of these are elderly folk who have suffered strokes which have taken away speech and left paralysed limbs. Communication is often very difficult and it is hard to understand what they are trying to say. Frustration at not being able to make oneself understood often brings tears from the patient and calls for a lot of love and patience in return.

Several of these dear folk are living a type of second childhood too, and I spent a lot of time wrapping up a doll for one lady who crooned to it and called it "my baby".

Room after room, upstairs and down, accommodate dozens of people whose greatest problem is old age and the incapacity which it brings. The hospital I have the privilege to visit is only one of hundreds which exist in the country. No doubt the problems, difficulties and trials are all very similar but we thank God for the provision of dedicated staff who are akin to ministering angels upon earth. How they need our prayers and support; and how those patients need a visit! It is so easy to forget that their situation today can be ours tomorrow and not one of us would wish to be cast off like an old unwanted garment; "Therefore," says Jesus, "all things whatsoever ye would that men should do to you, do ye even so to them: for this is the law and the prophets."

18

THE POP FESTIVAL

I GET ACCUSTOMED to young folk bursting into my three Mission Youth Clubs with a dramatic or interesting story to tell. Over the years I have been greeted with the news of one lad being killed on his motor bike, another stabbed on a railway station and a third shot a doorman at a dance. Even those incidents failed to produce the buzz of excited conversation which equalled the news of the prospect of a pop festival just two miles away from one of the Clubs.

August 1975 saw a couple of weeks of Pop Festival at Watchfield, a village lying off the A420 about eight miles from Swindon and twenty miles from Oxford.

None of my youngsters had ever been to a pop festival but memories of the Isle of Wight and Reading festivals as seen on the television and reported in the press were still uppermost in their minds. Immediately the conversation swung round to people walking about naked, drugs, sex and pop music.

A tremendous amount of local controversy preceded the pop festival. Many of the villagers were frightened and concerned that with an influx of thousands of young pop fans would come a wave of violence and vandalism. Some said the local young folk would be influenced to take up drugs or sleep around, whilst others feared their property would be damaged or their vegetables stolen.

There were public meetings of protest. The local Member of Parliament was bombarded with questions and the District Council and several other interested bodies all got involved. Pressure was brought to bear to have the pop festival cancelled or transferred elsewhere, but the organisers pressed on. It was not very long before it became abundantly clear that the pop festival was going on as planned and water pipes and toilet facilities began to appear on the site.

The Ministry of Defence once had a Military Camp at Watchfield but it was now closed and the deteriorating huts and buildings and adjoining airstrip were considered ideal for the squatting pop fans. Acres of grassland surrounding the huts would accommodate the fans, the pop music stands and the hundreds of tents and bonfires that were expected.

On a Sunday, a week before the pop festival was due to commence, I found myself planned to preach at a Methodist Church about six miles away from the site. After the service I called at the home of friends who promptly showed me their greenhouse and supplied me with a very large bag of home-grown tomatoes. Thus laden I set off for home but I had only driven a couple of miles when I came across a couple of teenage hitch-hikers thumbing a lift.

I stopped to pick up a girl who was walking very slowly with bare feet just showing beneath her ankle-length dress. She was heavily weighed down with several baskets and a rolled up sleeping bag. Her campanion, looking very much like John Lennon, was similarly laden carrying a sleeping bag and a guitar and a tent was slung across his shoulders.

"We love you forever," he said with a grin and threw his arms open wide as I stopped and slid the minibus door open for the couple to get in.

The girl smiled and asked if I was going anywhere near the pop festival site and straightaway I realised the first-comers were on their way.

I agreed to a little detour in order to take my hitch-hikers right to the area, more out of curiosity and somehow because I had become quite fascinated with their breezy chatter.

When we arrived at the site there didn't appear to be much sign of life. I drove through an open gateway and along an old runway. Running parallel to this was a line of water pipes interspersed with taps and rows of temporary toilets.

We headed for a tall brick building which dwarfed a concrete hut from which flutered a white flag, and in the gathering gloom we could just discern about a dozen young people sitting around a smoky fire.

I was more than interested now and as I drew near to the group I was very conscious of their stares. I was determined to meet them, however, and knew there would be no better opportunity than this of delivering a couple of the fans.

A dozen faces peered up at me as I drew near to the fire. One young fellow sat strumming a guitar and another made an adjustment to a can of water boiling on a piece of tin at the edge of the blaze.

"Hiya," I said, hoping I sounded more casual than I felt, and one of the fellows at the fireside thrust a large tyre in my direction and with a downward motion of the hand indicated I should sit. I did so wishing that I wasn't wearing a suit and wondered if I should explain that I had just come from taking a service. I decided to sit, watch, and listen.

A tall girl, about twenty years of age, suddenly emerged from one of the huts carrying a pile of slices of bread. She was as brown as a berry and very attractive and wore a yellow blouse over a pair of old jeans. She went swiftly and silently around the group handing each one of us a slice of bread in turn.

"Haven't we got any butter?" asked one of the older men of the group, punctuating his sentence with obscenities, and spat a large piece of the bread into the fire.

The girl replied with a lot more obscene words and was swift to point out that there were no local shops open where she could buy butter on a Sunday.

As I sat there holding my piece of bread, I remembered the large bag of tomatoes my friends had given me earlier that evening. Without a word I walked over to the minibus and collected them and handed them around the group.

Without doubt that large bag of tomatoes was my passport to the circle because they all began talking to me at once and started to ask questions. I soon discovered that they were expecting a reporter from the "Daily Express" and they had already decided I was him. They all seemed relieved when I explained I was a local evangelist and someone muttered, "we always get some of you nuts at a festival".

"Have you got any more tomatoes, mister?" an unmistakable American voice came over my shoulder and I turned to see a small lad, about five years of age, looking at me. He only wore a pair of shorts and his chest, arms and face were covered with streaks of green and silver paint.

The fellow playing the guitar offered the lad his tomato since I had none left, and I noticed the youngster stagger around the fire for it.

"Let's play the guitar," he said and the owner obligingly handed it over. "Be careful with it then," the guitarist went on and then exclaimed, "You've been drinking again. You're drunk!"

"I've only had some cider," was the very slurred reply and it was only then I understood that the child was drunk. He strummed on the instrument for a few moments and then sat with it across his knees until finally he got up with some difficulty and walked round the back of me.

Without any warning whatsoever I suddenly felt a terrific blow on the back of the head, which nearly knocked me for six. "That's for not saving me a tomato," the kid said and I was vaguely aware that he had hit me with all his might with the guitar.

"Come on to bed," the girl said, and after much swearing spitting and punching, the little chap was dragged away.

Still sitting by the fire I asked about the festival, numbers expected, groups appearing and so on. I very soon felt at home because these people were extremely friendly, even if their language was colourful.

By the time I left I had been allocated space in a hut to put my "church stuff and grub in" as it was called, and a lad called Daz promised me faithfully he would look after my things. It was a good job I didn't take Daz at his word, for on my subsequent visits to the site I never saw him again and I found my space had been taken over by a double sleeping bag, a card-board box and a candle.

The following night I was back on the site again and met some more interesting folk. A few had erected smallish tents but most of the newcomers had decided on something more substantial in the huts or large hangar type buildings.

A girl and two lads had moved into a small room in one of the larger buildings. It had no windows but between them the trio had painted windows and curtains on the walls. Shelves bearing plates, cups and saucers all in artistry adorned those walls too, also pictures of chairs and flowers. A mat had been painted in the doorway with the word WELCOME on it and the outside walls were ablaze with painted butterflies. I was astonished at so much art work undertaken in so short a time. It was really beautiful and very professional looking.

I was warmly received as I admired the handiwork and soon we were talking about war and friendship, hypocrites and folk who really care for others. One of these young men asked me to define what an evangelist was and what was the difference between being a Christian and religious. I told them about my work with the problem youth in three Mission Youth Clubs and said I thought practical Christianity was very important. They all agreed.

During the week scores of folk appeared at Watchfield. Beardies, hippies, straight guys, kids, teenagers and middle-aged with tents, motor bikes, old bangers, guitars and women. They came from all over Britain, some from America and quite a lot from the Continent. There were different nationalities and a diversity of backgrounds but I found two striking factors – the first was the closeness of the relationship one with another and the second, the common passion for pop music.

I visited the pop festival nine times in all, and on each occasion I was warmly received. Scores of youngsters listened to the gospel and accepted Scripture tracts. It was an experience I shall never forget.

I spent hours sitting with groups around camp fires and I was deeply touched by the sense of sharing and caring. I never once attached myself to a group without being offered some item of food or drink, and I had the impression that the whole affair was like one gigantic family gathering.

Whenever a newcomer arrived at a fireside someone always asked him if he had a tent or if he needed something to eat. I had never before or since witnessed so much concern for one another, as tents were open to strangers and often became overcrowded.

One night I offered some chocolate to a group and they accepted it only on the grounds that I took half a tin of cold beans in exchange for it. I drank endless cups of coffee, some sweetened with honey and more often than not without milk.

There were moments of sensationalism when someone appeared to walk about in the nude or girls appeared on the scene bare breasted. These things were simply accepted and no ribald comments were made or undue attention taken.

Music blared from hastily erected stands and groups of fans both large and small sat or stood on the grass near them. Couples danced, kissed and got themselves entwined and many just entertained each other in small communities.

I came across quite a lot of drug-taking and this bothered me. Pills were openly shared and three or four times I was asked for the junk. It was obvious from the glazed eyes and dead pan faces that shone in the firelight that a good number were spacing out or taking a trip, but, the subject hardly ever came up as a topic for conversation.

Throughout each evening I wandered from group to group just sitting and listening to the music with fans. I joined in conversations and deliberately brought these around to spiritual things and witnessed for God where it was possible.

I lost count of the times I was asked to continue when I fell silent after quoting something from the Bible. Everywhere it seemed as though the kids were looking for spiritual answers to lifes problems, as though everything else had failed and this was something new they had not yet tried.

I listened to some amazing stories and answered endless questions but my heart was burdened with the biggest question of all. Who really loved and cared for these kids apart from God?

Personal stories were poured out to me and I in turn was taking these to God in prayer in the early hours of each morning. I told Him about Nicky, Janice, Barry and many others.

Nicky was seventeen and a Londoner. He sat crouched between a gang of us around a large bonfire, his hands cupped around a tin mug of steaming coffee. I noticed how he stared into the fire and spoke very quietly, as almost to himself.

"I hopped school eighteen months ago," he began, "me parents had split and neither of them wanted me. Nine times out of ten I would go home at night and there would be a police car outside our house. My old man kept coming back to the old dear and finding her with fellows, then there would be a scrap and the neighbours would go for the fuzz."

The whole group was listening now and Nicky continued, "The constant rows got on me nerves so I went up North to some friends. I hitch-hiked as far as Warrington and met up with a mate who was roaming too. He was going to a concert at Manchester and we travelled on together. We stuck together for three months after that and then he went off to Germany and I travelled on my own for a bit."

"I got a job, two in fact, but they were both 'inside' jobs and I like to be out, so I pushed on until I got home again. Then I had the shock of me life, my old dear had scarpered and a bunch of Greeks were living in our flat." Nicky fell silent.

"What happened then, Nicky?" I asked, "did you find out where your mother had gone?"

"No," he replied, "I didn't have a clue where she was until I came to this festival six days ago. I was going across to the chip van and I met a kid I used to go to discos with in London, he was always at our place and I went to his. I asked him if he knew where the old dear had gone and he didn't but he said his old lady would know and I should 'phone her. Well I did 'phone her because I wanted to get in touch with my old gal again, I wanted to pick up me bank book you see, because its got about twenty quid in it and I wanted me big Union Jack to fix on the tent."

At this point Nicky threw the remaining half a mug of coffee into the fire and he swore as it hissed and caused it to smoke. He seemed annoyed now and muttered viciously, "Hell, what does it matter anyway?"

"Go on," I urged, "did you trace your Mum?"

"Yes, and a fat lot of good it did me," Nicky went on, "me mate's mother gave me my old lady's 'phone number so I rang her up, and said I would be calling for me bank book and flag." "Don't bother," she said all sarcastic like, "I am going to Jersey with a friend and after that I am going to be very busy and it will not be convenient for you to come."

Turning to me, Nicky looked at me straight in the eye and there were large tears in his. "So you see," he said, "nobody wants me, there's not a soul in this world who cares whether I live or die, and you're only pretending to be interested."

"No, I am interested Nicky or I wouldn't sit and listen to you," I said, "the very reason I am here is to tell you that Jesus loves you, so great is His love that He died for you. Jesus said, 'This is My commandment, that ye love one another, as I have loved you. Greater love hath no man than this, that a man lay down his life for his friends. Ye are my friends, if ye do whatsoever I command you.'"

I then proceeded to explain to the little group and Nicky in particular, how Christ loved them, how He died for sins on the Cross and then rose from the dead. I went on to tell them how He continues to love and answer prayer, to give power and purpose for living, and each listener hung on to every word in deep silence. They were hungering for the Word of God, and I believe several were fed with new hope when I concluded with words from Jeremiah, "The Lord hath appeared of old unto me, saying, Yea, I have loved thee with an everlasting love;

therefore with loving kindness have I drawn thee." I didn't leave Nicky until I told him that Christ would never forsake him and that he could know Him as a friend that sticketh closer than a brother. Later his broad grin assured me that he understood and I knew God was getting through.

One night I was walking along the runway when a noisy old car overtook me. Above the noise of the car I could hear hysterical screaming and shouting and I wondered whether someone was being raped or high on drugs. I didn't have to wonder for long because seconds later, in the darkness, I saw a huddled figure thrown out of the car which was travelling at speed.

I ran to the body which was lying, quivering, face down on the runway. The girl in her early twenties, was crying softly and kept muttering, "the sod! the sod!"

Slowly she rose to her feet and her face was a mess. She had two black eyes, a swollen upper lip and she kept dabbing at a bleeding nose with the back of her hand.

"Are you all right?" I asked and could have kicked myself for asking such a daft question.

"Yeah," she replied, "the old man and I have had a bit of a go. He's stoned out of his mind and he's nicked that car. The coppers are already looking for him and if he gets picked up tonight, he'll go down for sure."

By this time her nose was pouring with blood and I suggested that I should take her to the nearest tap for a clean-up. In the darkness we found a water pipe together and followed it along until we came across another girl on her knees striking matches beneath a tap. The second girl had washed her hands and in the process had dropped a ring. She was kneeling on a patch of wet gravel and mumbled to herself as she searched. It was sometime before I could figure out what she was doing because she was incoherent through drink and was retching all the time.

I found that my bleeding companion was called Janice and the girl on her knees was Jean; and in no time at all they were trying to help each other whilst I searched for the ring by match light until I found it.

Janice cupped her hands beneath the tap and gently dabbed at her bruised face with the cold water; and all this time she was expressing concern about her husband and his prospect of getting picked up by the police.

I said I was surprised that she was so concerned about him, in view of the way he had beaten her up and dumped her, and she replied, "Well I love him, don't I?"

Here was one who knew literally how to turn the other cheek and I was the one to learn a lesson that night. Janice was prepared to go on loving a fellow who was constantly giving her stress and pain but she never once complained for herself. "I'll pray for you," I said as I left Janice with Jean at the latter's tent by the water pipe, and handed them both a tract on the subject of God's love. I pray that both will find that love.

Very late one evening I called at the Krishna building where several youngsters were in meditation surrounded by coloured tapestries. Coffee and other refreshments were being handed out and there appeared to be an atmosphere of complete peace. It was a vivid contrast to the noise of the pop groups which were quite a long way away. The Krishna silence was followed by a chant and voices rose and fell in unison, so that it attracted quite a few of the fans. One of the fans, who later I discovered was called Barry, was very interested in Krishnaism and I was interested in his comments contrasting this worship to that of the Christian Church. I was rather sad, however, that he left the group before I had a chance to speak to him, since I felt he was seeking after a faith.

A few days later I attended the annual meeting of the Soldiers' and Airmen's Scripture Readers Association at the Baptist Church in Wantage. At the close of the service a Christian friend asked me to have a word with a young man who had crept in at the back of the church. He had come in to avoid a terrific thunderstorm and he was cold and hungry.

My friend took me to meet the young man and it was no less

than Barry whom I had met earlier at Watchfield. The pop festival was a talking point straightaway, and because he was without money and hungry I invited him out for a meal. Whilst we ate I discovered that Barry had got himself a job fruit picking at Harwell. He was living in a small hut which he shared with bales of hay and fruit. The hut had been kindly put at his disposal by his employer.

Barry had expected to receive his wages on the Saturday I met him at the church, but he explained that to his disappointment he had found the wages were not paid until Mondays for casual labourers. This practice ensured that there was a labour force on Monday mornings and the labourers didn't disappear over the weekend.

There was little Barry could do without money so he chose to go into Wantage and wander around the fair which was there that weekend. The sudden thunderstorm had driven the lad into church because he had no money to visit the pubs or the cafe.

After we had eaten I offered to take the young fellow home but he insisted on me driving him to his little hut instead. He had all his clothes there and he wanted to be near his work.

We talked freely of many things on the six mile drive to Harwell and then spent over an hour sitting and chatting in my minibus. We started at Krishna and ended up talking about God, Jesus Christ, prayer and miracles. I also found that Barry had left a good professional job before he started roaming and the reason for this was that his wife had left him. Even so, he spoke of her and his children with nothing but love and showed me their photographs which he treasured.

I couldn't help thinking that if Barry's wife could hear his words of love, her attitude would be different.

Perhaps our attitude to God would be different too if we listened to His words of love because He says, "As the Father hath loved me, so have I loved you: continue ye in my love. If ye keep my commandments, ye shall abide in my love; even as I have kept my Father's commandments, and abide in His love.

These things have I spoken unto you, that my joy might remain in you, and that your joy might be full."

Before I left Barry I got his assurance that he would have Sunday lunch with my mother and me the following day. I picked him up and we continued our chat on spiritual things. I was very pleased when he asked if he could go to Sunday School where I was to teach that afternoon; then after tea he went out with me again, as I was due to preach at a church some distance away. As we travelled back to Barry's little hut at the end of the day I sensed that he was very happy and a lot more relaxed. It did not come as any surprise when he asked for a lift to one of the Mission Youth Clubs the following night.

This type of pattern followed for a month. Each Sunday Barry came to lunch and he attended the Mission Youth Clubs through the week and we offered him such hospitality as we could. In return Barry tinkered with my minibus and carried out all sorts of repairs, but what touched me most of all was his contribution to our Harvest Thanksgiving.

Unbeknown to me this young man had gone to his employer and asked if he could have some of the pears and plums he was picking for the Thanksgiving. Barry told me how upset he was when the employer said he could have some of the fruit which had fallen off the trees. "It seems terrible to me," he said, "that God who provided the fruit in the first place cannot have it straight from the tree but it has to be picked up off the ground." I assured him that God understood and would bless him because he was giving all he had. How like the poor widow in the Scripture who threw two mites, which equalled one farthing, into the temple treasury. The rich folk gave much but Jesus said, "This poor widow hath cast more in than all they which have cast into the treasury: For all they did cast in of their abundance; but she of her want did cast in all that she had, even all her living."

As I was getting ready for service that evening, Barry was at the sink carefully washing and drying each individual pear and plum in turn; then he arranged them carefully for display in a box.

The lengthy process of washing and drying and polishing each piece of fruit was filling me with impatience as I envisaged arriving late at the church where I was to take the service. "Come on, Barry," I urged, "you have not got time to wash it all, put it in the box as it is!"

I shall never forget the look in his eyes and the way he quietly replied, "The Lord deserves the best," as he continued to wash and wipe every pear and plum.

As I looked upon the box of fruit which Barry had sacrificed, I couldn't help thinking of the fruit of our lips and the way God views our sacrifices. In the book of Hebrews we are reminded, "by Him (Christ) therefore let us offer the sacrifice of praise to God continually, that is, the fruit of our lips giving thanks to His name. But to do good and to communicate forget not: for with such sacrifices God is well pleased." I felt sure that what Barry had just said and what he was offering was going to be received by God and I prayed that Barry in turn would receive Him.

Four weeks later the fruit picking came to an end and so the time came for Barry to move on. We had marvellous conversation concerning the Lord and it was a very great joy to be able to pray with him. He promised to call and see us again when he was in the area and although I have not seen him since, I am convinced we shall meet again.

The pop festival brought me very little sleep during those nine days, it was hard and tense work calling for a lot of grace and tact but the Lord was my strength. I experienced the reality of two verses from the Scripture – Nehemiah 8:10 and Isaiah 40:31, "For the joy of the Lord is your strength," and "They that wait upon the Lord shall renew their strength; they shall mount up with wings as eagles; they shall run, and not be weary; and they shall walk, and not faint."

During the pop festival I came across a number of other Christians who were witnessing to their personal faith in the Lord Jesus Christ. Some were testifying that they had once been hooked on drugs but Christ had set them free. "Therefore if any man be in Christ, he is a new creature: old things are passed away; behold, all things are become new." (2 Corinthians 5:17.)

Others were showing gospel films on a large screen. It was easy to see the pictures but difficult to hear the dialogue, for the volume of the pop music. But, all things considered, I wonder who learnt the most? The pop fans from the Christians or the Christians from the fans?

For my part I learnt a lot about love in action and considering others less fortunate than myself. The fans showed me that there was a very large vacuum to be filled in their lives, a vacuum which was not being filled by so called freedom, drink, drugs, sex or music. I pray that some of them at least found Christ alone could fill that vacuum where all else failed.

The message of the gospel never changes, "For the Son of man is come to seek and to save that which was lost" "And the lord said unto the servant, Go out into the highways and hedges, and compel them to come in, that my house may be filled."

Through each moment I spent at the pop festival my heart's desire was that fans would turn on to Jesus. There I could see them sitting by candle-light in the night, but longed and prayed that they would accept Christ The Light of the World and be prepared for that great day when He will call His elect to Heaven. I could see Heaven as a kind of wonderful festival that went on for all eternity because in the last Chapter of the Bible I had read, "And there shall be no night there; and they need no candle, neither light of the sun; for the Lord God giveth them light: and they shall reign for ever and ever." Amen.

19

DAILY BREAD

"IT IS DARK when we go to work and it's dark when we come home again," my colleague grumbled good naturedly. "The only time we see our homes in daylight is at weekends." The complaint was true enough. I leave home at 6.30 a.m., five days a week, to catch a coach to my Civil Service job twenty six miles away. It is 5.15 p.m. by the time we get home, so we leave and return to our homes in darkness during the winter months. Even so, I am grateful for the transport which is provided by the Government Department where I work because this ensures that I get one and a half hours relaxation on the coach during a normal seventeen or eighteen hour day.

Apart from more than fifty miles of travelling daily and my full time secular office job, there is something to do for the Lord every day of the week. During each period of seven days there are three evenings of problem youth work in separate village Mission Youth Clubs. On the days when the Clubs are not open there is still work to be done in connection with them, there are letters to be written to Courts or to members in prison or hospital. Then there are visits to these places and to homes, house to house visiting with the distribution of a newsletter and preparation for services, rallies and epilogues.

In the course of a week there are two meetings for children, a Sunday School and a Good News Club, a monthly visit to a geriatric hospital and preaching appointments somewhere every Sunday and often in the week. The ministry takes me to various parts of the country, so there is a lot of travelling involved too.

I am fortunate in that my employment offers me about six weeks holiday a year, including the Bank Holidays. I can take this at any time I choose, a single day at a time or a longer period if required. In this way I am able to conduct Christian Missions and travel farther afield to preach at services or to undertake deputation work for Mission for Christ, a ministry of rural evangelism. I do not take a personal holiday as such but incorporate a change and a little rest whilst still serving the Lord.

Within this very busy schedule I still find time to do the odd job around the home, write for Christian publications and follow my love for amateur dramatics. I am very amused, therefore, when I hear folk constantly complaining that they have not had time to complete something, when in fact they have much more time than I have. I am always being asked how I fit everything in without appearing to rush about like a scalded cat. Well, I believe that with God's help anyone can do what they want to do. If you are really led of the Holy Spirit to do something, the necessary time, grace and determination will be given. The reason so many fail to complete, or even undertake to do a task, is not really due to lack of time but is an excuse for not wanting to do that thing in the first place. Folk can always find time to do what they want to do.

I never cease to be amazed how individuals in congregations begin to fidget and look at their watches when one single hour of worship has expired. But watch the same person at the cinema, theatre or a football match and you will see no trace of the apparent rush to get home, even if the event goes on for three or four hours.

Most of us need a good shake-up in our attitude to God and His service, especially on the subject of giving to His work. God, who has given us all things richly to enjoy often gets a poor response from us.

We will indulge in all kinds of personal luxuries without a thought of the cost, but are we not sometimes guilty of taking out a handful of money and slipping in the smallest coin when the collecting plate comes to us? This is a serious matter to God, for in Malachi, Chapter 3 we read, "Will a man rob God? Yet ye have robbed me. But ye say, Wherein have we robbed thee? In tithes and offerings. Ye are cursed with a curse: for ye have robbed me, even this whole nation."

Then God goes on to say something very special. "Bring ye all the tithes into the storehouse, that there may be meat in mine house, and prove me now herewith, saith the Lord of hosts, if I will not open you the windows of heaven, and pour you out a blessing, that there shall not be room enough to receive it."

I think we all agree that we would like to enjoy overflowing blessing like that; well it is possible, because God urges us to prove Him here and now. Jesus said, "Where your treasure is, there will your heart be also," if we give beggarly, then we can expect barreness of soul. On the other hand, if we give liberally, our experience will be to receive "good measure, pressed down, and shaken together and running over". We can never out-give God who gave all for us.

I have found a very valuable secret as far as my prayer life is concerned. Too often my prayers were dictating to God what He should do. In every prayer I have learnt first to praise Him, then confess sin and claim forgiveness through His Cleansing Blood and then lay my petitions before Him. In each prayer I ask God if it may please Him to heal somebody or bless an individual in some way and conclude by praying that His will, not mine, be done. In every case the prayers are in the Name of Jesus, for He alone has the power to answer prayer.

It is, of course, essential to pray believing prayer and not be like the man who prayed for a fine day for the Sunday School outing and then made sure he didn't leave his umbrella behind! Jesus said, "Therefore I say unto you, what things soever ye desire, when ye pray, believe that ye receive them, and ye shall have them."

Claim God's promises. I accept the Bible as His inspired Word and every one of His promises in it I take as His written guarantee. I remember that God never changes and the miracles of old are still possible today.

Expect great things. God did great things for Abraham,

Moses, the prophets and the apostles. He is my God too and so He is able to do great things for me. I believe the tremendous things He has done and is doing in my life are due to the fact that I have learnt never to doubt His power. But to do this it is needful for me to be emptied of self in order to be filled with Him. This involves daily confession of sin and seeking new power for each task. If Christ is honoured first in a life, all other necessary things will be added. If He be lifted up in my preaching and witness, He will draw men and women unto Himself.

We shall win souls for God when we allow Him to do the work and have His will in our lives. The servant is not greater than his Lord and too frequently we seem to want to do the work of the Holy Spirit ourselves. Such a work will utterly fail and surely fall. The Psalmist says, "Except the Lord build the house, they labour in vain that build it." Bearing this in mind, I want the Lord only to be the builder of my life and ministry, and thus founded on Him, the solid Rock, I shall stand firm for time and eternity.

In His strength and in His Name I press on as Paul describes in Philippians, Chapter 3, "I press toward the mark for the prize of the high calling of God in Christ Jesus."

As I press on in the Master's service I know I can expect trials and tribulations from the old enemy the devil. I shall need to wear the whole armour of God to thwart his attacks but with Christ, I am on the victory side.

I am thankful to God too for faithful Christian brothers and sisters who are loyal to Him and to this ministry. We stand united in our love for the Saviour and seek to serve Him wherever He leads.

The youth are looking for guidance, help and love, where else can they obtain it, but from Jesus? If the Lord wills I shall continue to teach some of the young folk to drive, like Mervyn, a recent convert who loves the Lord and now wants to become mobile for Him. What a change there is in this young man who once nearly lost his life in a motor-cycle accident through drinking, now desiring to drive for the One who saved him. This is conversion and the glory is the Lord's.

As God directs I shall go on preaching, travelling, witnessing to the famous, to the many and the few. His grace is sufficient for me and His strength is made perfect in my weakness. My living for the Lord is a one day at a time experience for I know I cannot claim any tomorrow, my future is in His hands. I simply ask that I may give God all the glory for what He has done for and through me. I can only give as He first gives to me and so my constant prayer to Our Father in Heaven must always be – "Give us this Day." I know He will!